IBM Cognos 10 Framework Manager

A comprehensive, practical guide to using this essential tool for modeling your data for use with IBM Cognos Business Intelligence Reporting

Terry Curran

BIRMINGHAM - MUMBAI

IBM Cognos 10 Framework Manager

First published: May 2013

Production Reference: 1150513

Published by Packt Publishing Ltd.
Livery Place
35 Livery Street
Birmingham B3 2PB, UK.

ISBN 978-1-84968-576-4

www.packtpub.com

Cover Image by Gareth J (garth123@hotmail.co.uk)

Credits

Author
Terry Curran

Reviewers
Larry D. Bob
Ramesh Parcha
Gnaneshwar

Acquisition Editor
Joanne Fitzpatrick

Lead Technical Editor
Susmita Panda

Technical Editors
Prasad Dalvi
Saumya Kunder
Worrell Lewis
Amit Ramdas

Project Coordinator
Amey Sawant

Proofreader
Aaron Nash

Indexer
Tejal Soni

Graphics
Ronak Dhruv

Production Coordinator
Prachali Bhiwandkar

Cover Work
Prachali Bhiwandkar

About the Author

Terry Curran gained an interest in computers while studying for his first degree in Biological Chemistry at the University of Kent. He went on to work as a computer operator for a national supermarket company.

After working for several years as a computer operator, he went to Brighton Polytechnic, leaving with a Higher National Diploma in Computer Studies. Upon completion of his studies, he worked as a computer advisor at the City of London Polytechnic, assisting staff and students with their computer problems, and providing support for the various database systems in use across the Polytechnic. After taking voluntary redundancy from this post, he proceeded to the University of Stirling where he gained an MSc in Software Engineering.

After graduating from the University of Stirling, Terry commenced working for a software consultancy company. While working for this company, Terry assisted with the writing of a software package for the publishing industry using Cognos PowerHouse. While working for this company, Terry gained experience in Business Intelligence Reporting tools, being asked to familiarize himself with Cognos Impromptu and PowerPlay in order to promote the use of these tools to clients.

After this company ceased trading, Terry embarked on a career as a freelance computer consultant and contractor, using his experience with Cognos PowerHouse, various computer systems and databases, and Cognos Impromptu and PowerPlay, and later Cognos 8 and Cognos 10.

Terry continues to work as a freelance Cognos Business Intelligence consultant and contractor, making use of his extensive knowledge and experience of IBM Cognos Business Intelligence Reporting. During the past 15 years, Terry has worked for a range of different industries including aviation, pharmaceuticals, insurance, logistics, and manufacturing to name a few.

Terry is currently working for Ultra Electronics Command and Control Systems as a freelance Cognos consultant.

Terry Curran was a technical reviewer for the book *IBM Cognos 8 Report Studio Cookbook, Packt Publishing*.

Acknowledgement

I would like to thank Packt Publishing for offering the opportunity to write this book.

I would like to thank my wife Joyce, and my sons Francis and Alexander for encouraging me to write this book.

I would also like to thank Julie Jones for putting up with me for the past year while we have been working together at Ultra Electronics.

About the Reviewer

Larry D. Bob is an Enterprise Business Intelligence Architect with The Boeing Company, supporting the Finance Organization. He has over 15 years of technical and consulting experience in the design and development of BI applications, five of those years as a Cognos consultant. He was awarded the Cognos CIO Leadership Award in 2005, the Cognos Performance Leadership Award in 2007, and the TDWI Best Practices Award in 2008. Larry became a TDWI-certified Business Intelligence Professional in 2011 and is currently leading projects using Text Natural Language Processing and Predictive Analytics.

Ramesh Parcha graduated in Mechanical Engineering from Gulbarga University and he has been working in the IT industry for over 13 years. Presently he is working at NTTDATA as a Project Manager.

He has been working with IBM Cognos BI Products since 2006.

Earlier he has worked with SETKHAM, SIS Inoftech, Dataformix Technologies, USA, and Marketstrat, USA.

He has worked as a reviewer on a Video course on *IBM Cognos 10 Report Studio* and the book *IBM Cognos 8 Report Studio Cookbook* by *Packt Publishing*.

It was great pleasure reviewing this book and I would like to thank Susmita Panda and Amey Sawant.

www.PacktPub.com

Support files, eBooks, discount offers and more

You might want to visit www.PacktPub.com for support files and downloads related to your book.

Did you know that Packt offers eBook versions of every book published, with PDF and ePub files available? You can upgrade to the eBook version at www.PacktPub.com and as a print book customer, you are entitled to a discount on the eBook copy. Get in touch with us at service@packtpub.com for more details.

At www.PacktPub.com, you can also read a collection of free technical articles, sign up for a range of free newsletters and receive exclusive discounts and offers on Packt books and eBooks.

http://PacktLib.PacktPub.com

Do you need instant solutions to your IT questions? PacktLib is Packt's online digital book library. Here, you can access, read and search across Packt's entire library of books.

Why Subscribe?

- Fully searchable across every book published by Packt
- Copy and paste, print and bookmark content
- On demand and accessible via web browser

Free Access for Packt account holders

If you have an account with Packt at www.PacktPub.com, you can use this to access PacktLib today and view nine entirely free books. Simply use your login credentials for immediate access.

Instant Updates on New Packt Books

Get notified! Find out when new books are published by following @PacktEnterprise on Twitter, or the *Packt Enterprise* Facebook page.

Table of Contents

Preface

IBM Cognos Framework Manager is a modeling tool for creating and managing business related metadata available in all Cognos Business Intelligence applications. It allows modelers to model relational data dimensionally, apply hierarchies to allow drill behaviors, apply member functions, and query any of the supported data sources (relational database with SQL or OLAP with MDX).

The main users of Framework Manager are data warehouse developers and data modelers. Report authors use the metadata information, which is set up using Framework Manager when creating new reports.

It is not a standalone product, but a core backend tool used to build a foundation for Query Studio, Report Studio, and Analysis Studio.

What this book covers

Chapter 1, Getting Started, provides an overview of the configuration of Framework Manager, including details of how to run Framework Manager, and the main features of the user interface.

Chapter 2, Proven Practice, covers the proven practices to use when you are designing a new data model in Framework Manager.

Chapter 3, Importing Data Sources, covers the details of the different types of data sources that Framework Manager can import, and how to import your data sources.

Chapter 4, Modeling Relational Data, covers the modeling of the relationships between the data tables. After importing your metadata you must ensure it meets your users' reporting requirements.

Chapter 5, Modeling Dimensional Data, covers the use of Dimensional Modeling - more correctly Dimensionally Modeled Relational data (DMR).

Chapter 6, Creating the Business and Presentation Layers, covers the creation of the Business and Presentation layers. The Business layers are layers where we add business rules to our model to make it more user friendly. The Presentation layer is what your report authors will see in Report Studio, Query Studio, and Analysis Studio.

Chapter 7, Creating and Publishing Packages, covers the creation and publishing of your packages. Once all the layers of the model have been created we have to present the model to your report authors for them to use.

Chapter 8, Maintaining Projects, covers the techniques for ensuring that changes to the data sources are reflected in your model. This chapter also covers the techniques to allow multi-user modeling.

Chapter 9, Model Design Accelerator, covers Model Design Accelerator, which simplifies the creation of relational star schema models. It will assist both novice and expert modelers to build Framework Manger models without needing extensive experience and training.

Chapter 10, Parameter Maps, covers Parameter Maps, which can be used to create conditional query subjects that allow for substitutions when a report is run.

Appendix, Data Warehouse Schema Map, shows details of the Schema Map for the Data Warehouse used in *Chapter 9, Model Design Accelerator*.

What you need for this book

To use the examples in this book you will need a copy of IBM Cognos Framework Manager, and this software is only available as a Microsoft Windows program.

All examples have been developed using IBM Cognos Framework Manager 10.1.1.

The examples in *Chapter 9, Model Design Accelerator*, will only work with IBM Cognos Framework Manager 10, since this was a new feature in IBM Cognos 10.

All other examples should work with any version of IBM Cognos Framework Manager.

To function correctly, Framework Manager requires a suitably configured IBM Cognos Business Intelligence Server. Many of the examples make use of the IBM Cognos Business Intelligence Samples, so the following software is also required:

- IBM Cognos Business Intelligence Server – this needs to be the same version as Framework Manager.
- A suitable webserver for example, Apache Webserver or Microsoft IIS.

- IBM Cognos Business Intelligence Samples – any version but preferably the same version as Framework Manager.
- SQL Server 2008 – to load the data used in *Chapter 9, Model Design Accelerator*, and as a suitable database for loading IBM Cognos Business Intelligence Samples.

Who this book is for

This book will be useful to all developers, both novice and expert, who use IBM Cognos Framework Manager to build packages for use by Report Studio, Query Studio, and Analysis Studio reports.

Readers are expected to have a basic understanding of reporting in IBM Cognos and are advised to get some hands-on experience of one or more Cognos studios. This book will only cover IBM Cognos Framework Manager.

Conventions

In this book, you will find a number of styles of text that distinguish between different kinds of information. Here are some examples of these styles, and an explanation of their meaning.

Code words in text are shown as follows: "Common session parameters that you may see include `account.personalInfo.email`, `account.personalInfo.firstname`, and `account.personalInfo.surname`."

A block of code is set as follows:

```
SELECT "product_name_lookup"."product_number" AS "PRODUCT_NUMBER",
```

New terms and **important words** are shown in bold. Words that you see on the screen, in menus or dialog boxes for example, appear in the text like this: "Go to **Start** | **All Programs** | **IBM Cognos 10** | **IBM Cognos Configuration**."

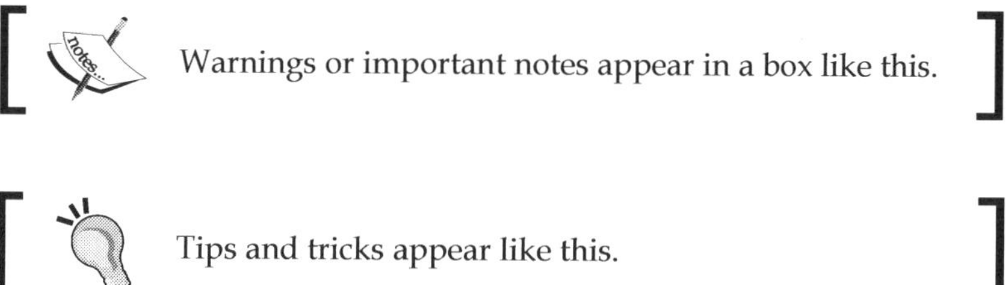

Warnings or important notes appear in a box like this.

Tips and tricks appear like this.

Reader feedback

Feedback from our readers is always welcome. Let us know what you think about this book—what you liked or may have disliked. Reader feedback is important for us to develop titles that you really get the most out of.

To send us general feedback, simply send an e-mail to `feedback@packtpub.com`, and mention the book title via the subject of your message.

If there is a topic that you have expertise in and you are interested in either writing or contributing to a book, see our author guide on `www.packtpub.com/authors`.

Customer support

Now that you are the proud owner of a Packt book, we have a number of things to help you to get the most from your purchase.

Errata

Although we have taken every care to ensure the accuracy of our content, mistakes do happen. If you find a mistake in one of our books—maybe a mistake in the text or the code—we would be grateful if you would report this to us. By doing so, you can save other readers from frustration and help us improve subsequent versions of this book. If you find any errata, please report them by visiting `http://www.packtpub.com/submit-errata`, selecting your book, clicking on the **errata submission form** link, and entering the details of your errata. Once your errata are verified, your submission will be accepted and the errata will be uploaded on our website, or added to any list of existing errata, under the Errata section of that title. Any existing errata can be viewed by selecting your title from `http://www.packtpub.com/support`.

Piracy

Piracy of copyright material on the Internet is an ongoing problem across all media. At Packt, we take the protection of our copyright and licenses very seriously. If you come across any illegal copies of our works, in any form, on the Internet, please provide us with the location address or website name immediately so that we can pursue a remedy.

Please contact us at `copyright@packtpub.com` with a link to the suspected pirated material.

We appreciate your help in protecting our authors, and our ability to bring you valuable content.

Questions

You can contact us at `questions@packtpub.com` if you are having a problem with any aspect of the book, and we will do our best to address it.

1
Getting Started

IBM Cognos Framework Manager is the metadata modeling development environment for IBM Cognos BI. It is available only as a Microsoft Windows client tool, which must first be installed and then configured.

This chapter does not cover the installation of Framework Manager as it is assumed that you would have already done this. This chapter covers only the settings to ensure that Framework Manager works successfully.

The topics covered in this chapter include:

- Basic configuration of Framework Manager
- Starting Framework Manager
- Framework Manager user interface

By the end of this chapter, you will have configured and have a working Framework Manager, and know what the basic features of the user interface are.

For this chapter, it may be useful to have the IBM Cognos Business Intelligence sample project installed or a Framework Manager project available.

Configuring Framework Manager

To configure Framework Manager or to confirm that your Framework Manager is correctly configured, go to **Start** | **All Programs** | **IBM Cognos 10** | **IBM Cognos Configuration**.

This will display the configuration screen:

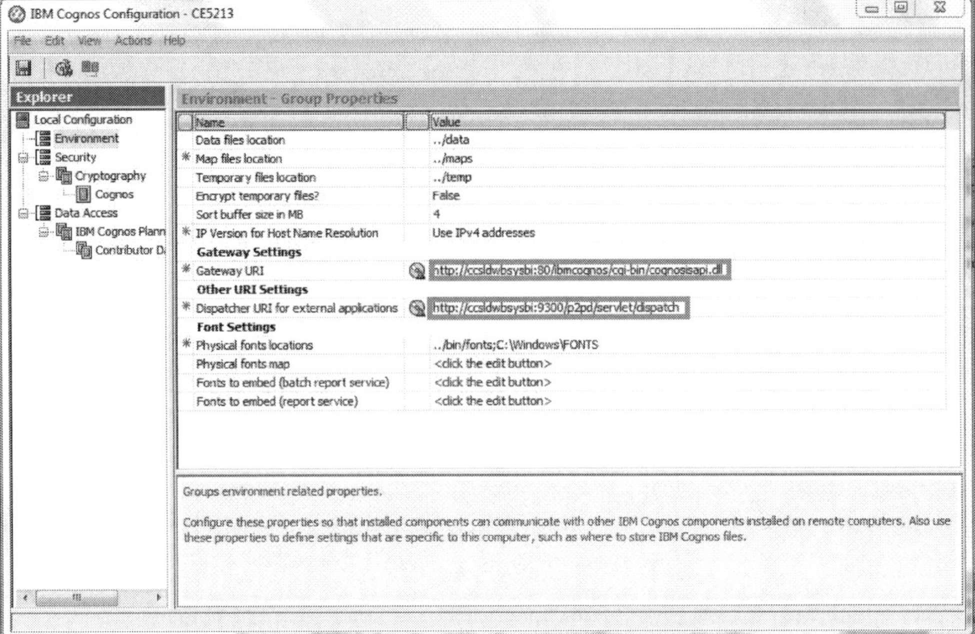

Now perform the following steps:

1. Select **Environment**.
2. Confirm the following values:
    - **Gateway URI**: This should be the same as the one used by the IBM Cognos Business Intelligence Server.
    - **Dispatcher URI for external applications**: This should be the same as the one used by the IBM Cognos Business Intelligence Server.

   Your Cognos administrator should be able to confirm the correct values to be used for your server.

3. If you make any changes, save your settings by clicking on the save icon on the toolbar or by selecting **File | Save and Exit Cognos Configuration**.

Starting Framework Manager

To start Framework Manager, go to **Start** | **All Programs** | **IBM Cognos 10** | **IBM Cognos Framework Manager**.

This will display the initial screen:

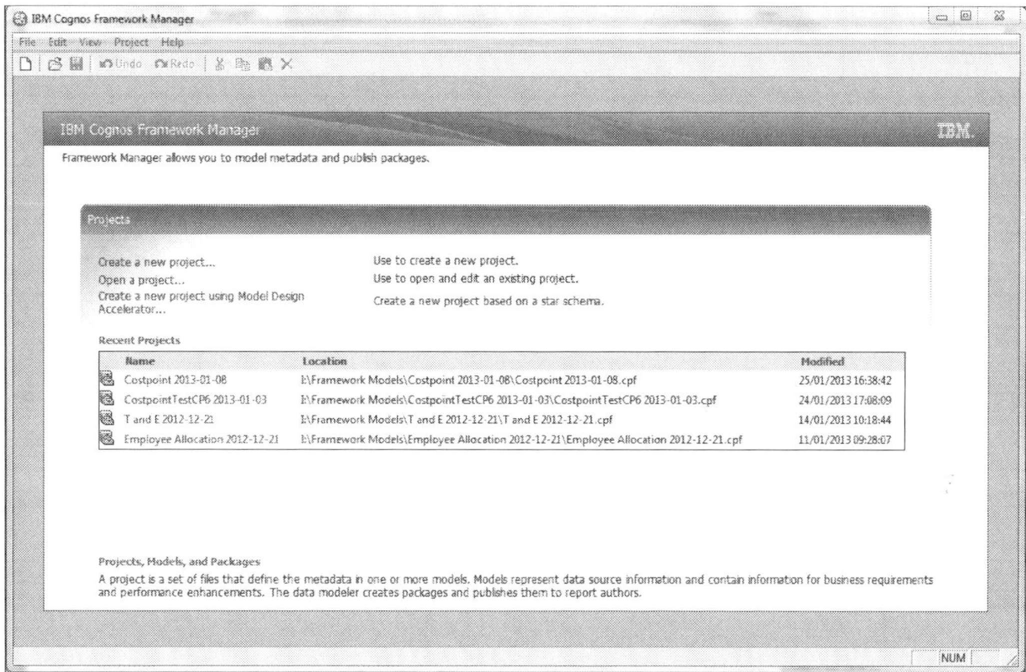

This screen shows the last four Framework Manager projects that you had opened, including information on the project location and the date when the project was last modified.

From this screen you can manage your projects in several ways.

From **File** | **Manage Projects**, you have the ability to:

- Copy a project
- Move a project
- Rename a project
- Delete a project

You have three options in the middle of the screen:

- Create a new project
- Open a project
- Create a new project using Design Accelerator

Alternatively, if you have already opened the project in a previous session, you can simply click on the project name to open the project.

A Framework Manager project appears as a folder that contains a project file (`.cpf`) and the specific `.xml` files that define the project. The project files usually consist of the following files:

- `Archive-log.xml`: Archive log messages file
- `Custom-data.xml`: Custom settings file
- `IDlog.xml`: Contains details for the diagram's display settings
- `Log.xml`: Project log file
- `Model.xml`: Project model file
- `Preferences.xml`: User preferences file
- `Session-log.xml`: Current session log file
- `Session-log-backup.xml`: Previous session log file
- `<project_name>.cpf`: Project control file

The files in the project folder are unique to each project.

All the project files are text files, and can be viewed and modified using any suitable text editor.

For now we will choose the option to open an existing project.

Click on **Open a project**, and then use the file explorer window to browse to the location of your project or the `samples` directory.

If you have installed the IBM Cognos Samples, the `samples` projects will be located at `C:\Program Files\ibm\cognos\c10\webcontent\samples\models`.

Or you can click on the title of the project that you have already been working on.

If your IBM Cognos Server requires authentication, you may be requested to log in. Enter your usual login credentials and Framework Manager will connect to the IBM Cognos Environment that you have previously configured.

User interface

Once you open the project, the main user interface screen is displayed:

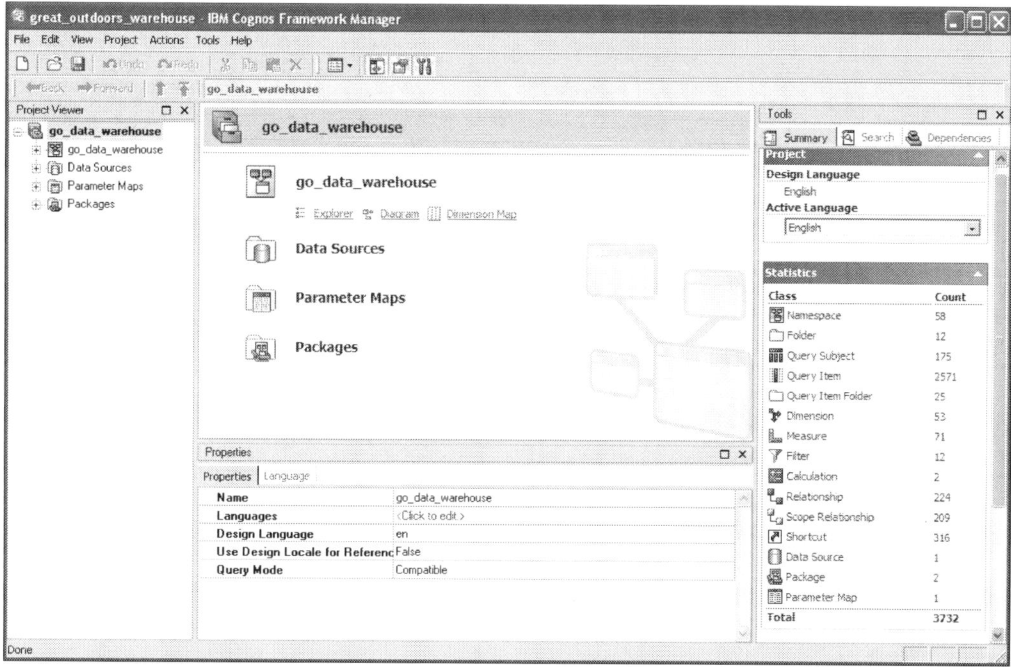

This is the project's work area, which shows an overview of the whole project. This page contains several additional panes that you can use to view and modify the objects in a project.

The main **Project** pane cannot be hidden or moved. The **Project Viewer**, **Tools**, and **Properties** panes can be hidden or detached and moved around the work area. If you hide a tool panel, it can be restored by using the **View** menu.

The Project Viewer pane

The **Project Viewer** pane shows the project in a hierarchical view. You can use the **Project Viewer** pane to view, modify, and create objects.

The **Project Viewer** pane uses various icons to represent different types of objects; these icons are described in more detail in the IBM Cognos documentation.

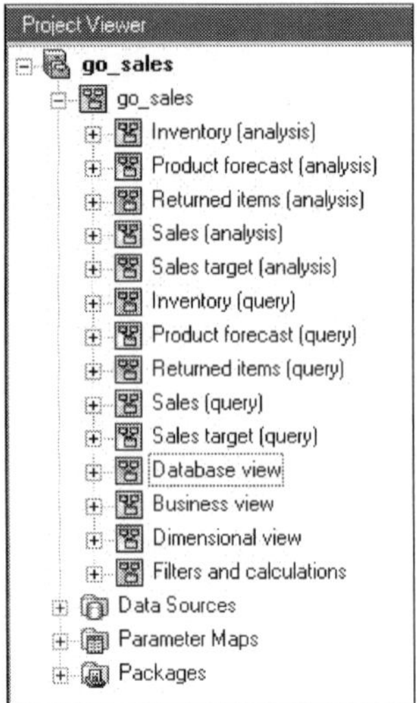

Within this pane, the main objects are grouped in the project model. The **Project Viewer** pane starts with the project at the top level; additional levels within the project may be expanded by clicking on the + sign beside each level.

Within the **Project Viewer** panel, you can find the following areas:

- **Data Sources**: These define the connection to external databases; a project can have one or more data sources defined
- **Parameter Maps**: These are similar to lookup tables and are discussed in more detail in *Chapter 10, Parameter Maps*
- **Packages**: These are the metadata definitions used by your report authors; they are discussed further in *Chapter 7, Creating and Publishing Packages*

The Explorer tab

The **Explorer** tab shows the contents of a project, similar to any filesystem. If you have a large number of objects in a project, it may be easier to locate them in the **Explorer** tab.

To go to the **Explorer** tab, click on the **Explorer** label in the central project work area.

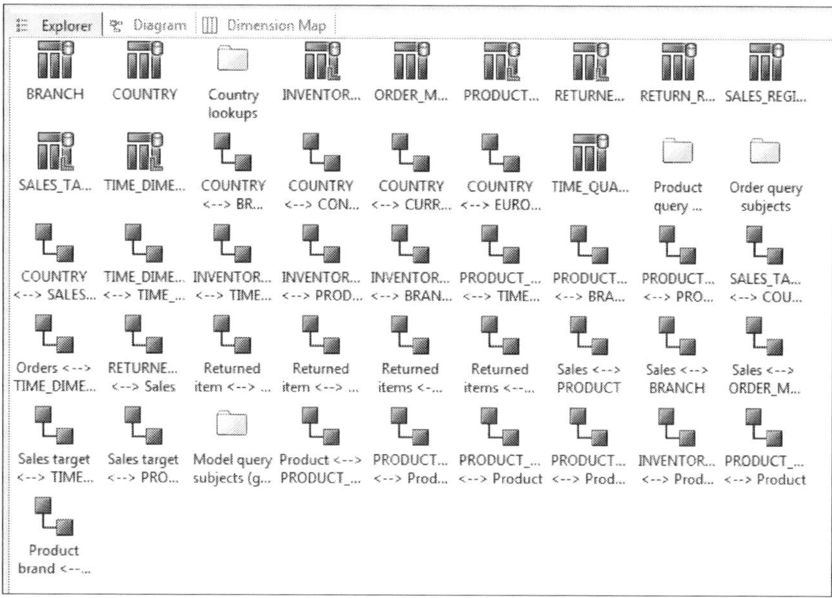

You can use the **Explorer** tab to view, create, and modify objects and relationships. You can also create folders and namespaces to group objects.

The Diagram tab

The **Diagram** tab shows the relationships between objects in a project.

To go to the **Diagram** tab, click on the **Diagram** label in the central project work area.

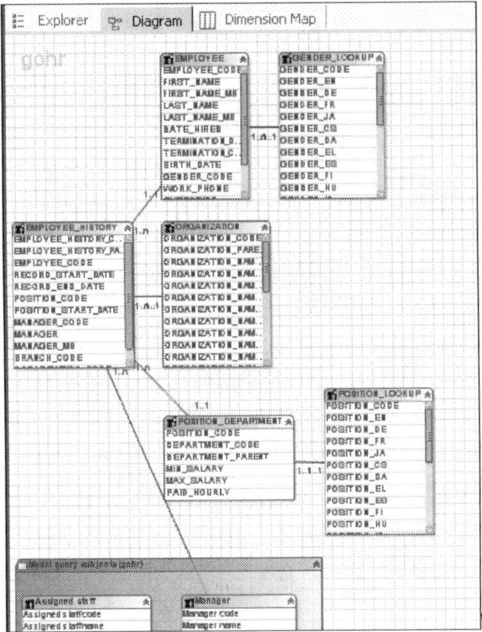

Relationships between the objects are shown with lines with cardinality notation. You can expand objects and namespaces to show the object hierarchy and the relationship between objects. In the **Diagram** tab, you can perform any of the following tasks:

- View, create, and modify objects and relationships.
- Create folders and namespaces to group objects.
- Change the settings for the diagrams.
- Change the layout of objects to either star layout or standard layout by navigating to **Diagram** | **Auto Layout**.
- Focus on an object by navigating to **Diagram** | **Set Focal Point**.
- Find an object by right-clicking on the object in **Project Viewer**, and clicking on **Locate** in **Diagram**.
- Zoom in or out by clicking on **Zoom** in **Diagram**.

- Expand or collapse all objects from the **Diagram** menu.
- Save the diagram for printing by navigating to **Diagram** | **Screen capture**, and specifying the name of the picture.
- Launch the Context Explorer by right-clicking on an object in the **Diagram** tab, and clicking on **Launch Context Explorer**.

[The Context Explorer is useful for quickly finding the relationships from a selected object.]

- Print the diagram in the Context Explorer by right-clicking on the Context Explorer background, and then clicking on **Print**. A **Print** button is also available from the Context Explorer toolbar. This menu also includes commands for previewing the diagram using **Print Preview** and changing page layout options using **Page Setup**.

The Dimension Map tab

The **Dimension Map** tab can be used to view, create, and modify hierarchies and levels for any dimension you have selected in **Project Viewer**. You can also view and modify the scope relationships.

To open the **Dimension Map** tab, click on the **Dimension** label in the central project work area:

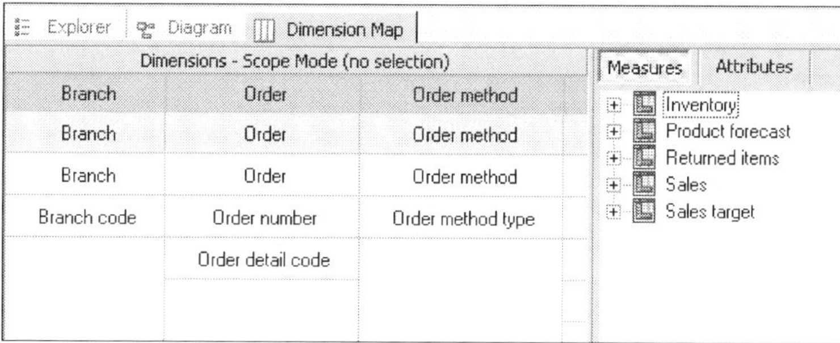

The **Measures and Attributes** tabs will be displayed after you click on the **Dimension Map** tab. The **Measures** tab can be used to view or modify all the measures and scope relationships that are available in the model. The **Attributes** tab can be used to view or modify the role of the selected query item.

The Properties pane

The **Properties** pane shows the properties of the object, or objects that you last selected in the other panes of the tabs within the panes.

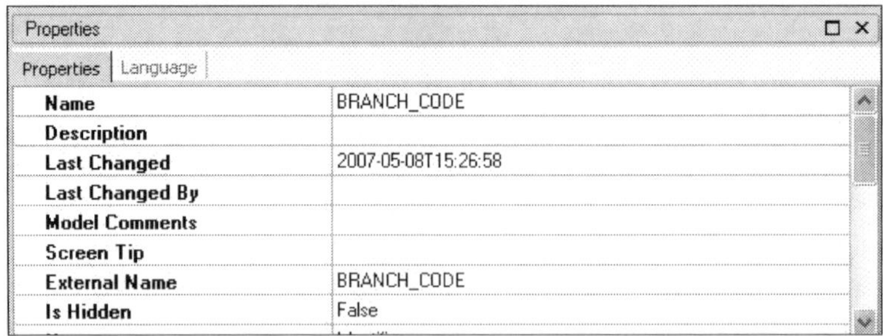

Default properties are set during import of your metadata, and some property values can later be modified during modeling. You can use the **Properties** pane to add, modify, or delete the properties of selected objects.

You can modify the properties for a single object or multiple objects at the same time.

Select multiple objects by pressing *Ctrl* and clicking on the items.

Framework Manager shows only the properties that are common to all the selected objects. You can apply a property value to multiple objects by clicking on the arrow to the right of the property and dragging the highlighted area over the properties to which you want to apply that value.

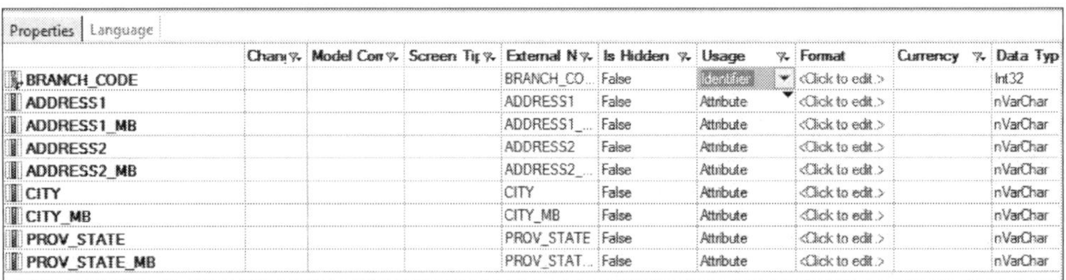

The Tools pane contains the Summary tab, the Search tab, and the Dependencies tab.

Hide the **Properties** pane when you do not need it, to provide more space on the screen.

The Tools pane

The **Tools** pane contains the **Summary** tab, the **Search** tab, and the **Dependencies** tab. The following screenshot show the **Tools** pane:

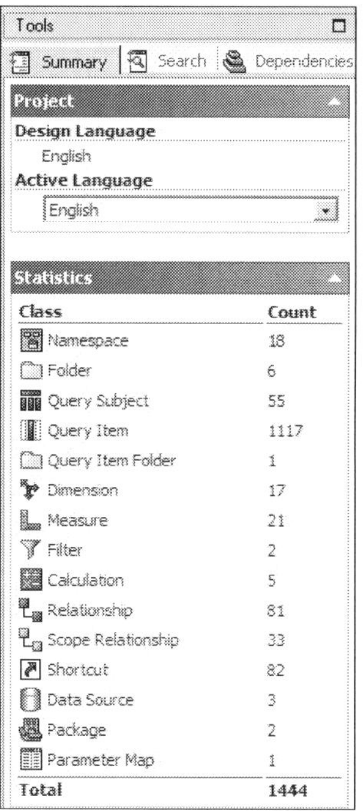

Hide the **Tools** pane when not needed, to provide more space on the screen.

The Summary tab

The **Summary** tab is divided into three sections. At the top, the **Project** section shows the design language and the active language. The design language is chosen at the start of a new project and cannot be changed; the active language may be changed by selecting a new language from the drop-down list.

The second section is the **Statistics** section. You can select any object from the **Project Viewer** to see various statistics about the chosen item. By default, if you do not select an item from the **Project Viewer**, the statistics are shown for the whole project.

The final section in the **Summary** tab shows actions that are available for the selected object.

The Search tab

When you have a large project open, it can sometimes be difficult to locate the items that you need. You can use the **Search** tab to quickly find any objects within your open model.

Enter the text you want to search for into the search box and click on the **Search** button.

The search is not case sensitive; you can use * and ? as wildcard characters to match multiple and single characters respectively.

Use the double down arrow button to expand the search to include things such as the following:

- **Condition**: For example, contains, does not contain, equals, not equal, and so on
- **Scope**: Where to start searching from
- **Class**: The type of item to search for, such as calculations, folders, and query items
- **Property**: The property to search for, such as data type, object name, and usage

By default the search uses the following criteria:

- **Condtion**: Contains
- **Scope**: The currently selected item (if nothing is selected, the whole project is selected)
- **Class**: All classes
- **Property**: All properties

The Dependencies tab

The **Dependencies** tab shows all the objects that are dependent on the selected item. To use the **Dependencies** tab, select any item from the **Project Viewer** pane, and drag-and-drop it to the upper pane of the **Dependencies** tab; all the dependent objects will be displayed in the lower pane of the **Dependencies** tab.

Toolbars

Some limited functionality is available through the toolbar. From the toolbar you can perform the following tasks:

- Create a new project
- Save a project that is currently open
- Open an existing project
- Copy and paste using the Windows clipboard
- Hide and show the **Project Viewer** pane, the **Properties** pane, and the **Tools** pane

You will probably find that the main functions used from the toolbar are to open and save projects.

Summary

By the end of this chapter, you should have a correctly configured Framework Manager.

You will have understood the main features of the user interface and the functioning of user interface items such as the project work area, the **Project View** pane, the **Properties** pane, the **Tools** pane, and the toolbar.

2

Proven Practice

This chapter covers ideas for best practices in creating your Framework Manager model.

The topics covered in this chapter include:

- Using namespaces to divide the model into layers
- Using folders within namespaces to provide logical grouping of data
- Renaming columns within tables, and use of shortcuts to allow the report designer to know where the data originates from
- Using Model Advisor to diagnose potential design problems

By the end of this chapter, you will have an understanding of the proven practices to use while designing a new data model in the Framework Manager.

Framework Manager is the modeling design tool used to model the metadata of your database to allow report authors to produce reports using the available reporting studios on the IBM Cognos BI reporting server.

Modeling layers

One of the basic principles of a good model design is to divide the model into a series of layers, each layer having a specific function within the model and a related set of modeling activities.

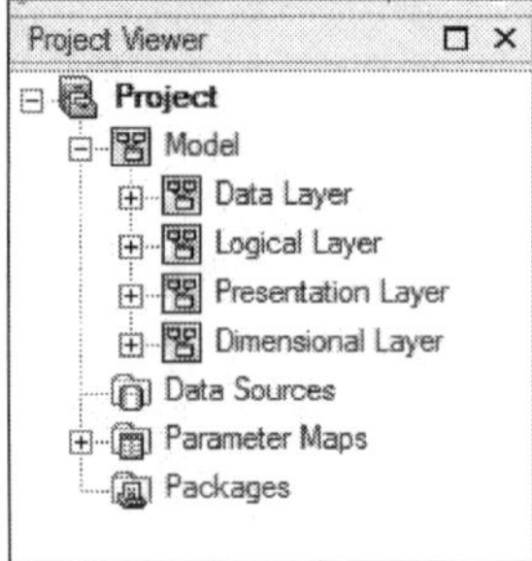

Originally IBM Cognos recommended the use of two layers, a data layer and a modeling layer. This was later refined by the inclusion of a Presentation layer, and a separate Dimensional layer if the **Dimensional Modeled Relational** (**DMR**) data is also used in the model.

The layers are built upon one another, with the lowest level being the data layer, the modeling layer as the middle layer, and the top layer being the presentation layer. The dimensional layer can be used to replace the presentation layer, or can be used in addition to the presentation layer.

Data layer

The data layer, also called the import layer, or the physical layer, contains the data source query subjects. This is directly based on the underlying database objects.

In order to retrieve the table information, you should use an unmodified query in SQL, similar to the following:

```
Select * from Table
```

This is the SQL command that the import process will generate for you. You can also modify this SQL command if required by adding filters or calculations. You will usually add joins, cardinality, and determinants at this level. For more information on joins, cardinality, and determinants see *Chapter 4, Modeling Relational Data*.

If you do not add any determinants, then the Framework Manager will add them automatically during the import process using the primary keys of the database table being imported.

Although there is nothing to prevent you from adding joins, cardinality, and determinants in any layer of the model, you should only add them in one layer of the model.

Some people recommend adding them in the data layer while others in the logical layer, so it's a matter of personal choice as to where these should be added.

Logical layer

The logical layer, sometimes also referred to as the modeling layer or the business layer, is where most of the modeling is likely to occur. It is used to provide business context and an understanding of the data objects in the data layer. Some of the required tasks include, but are not limited to the following:

- Combining elements from multiple tables to make more logical structures; for example, if you have an invoice header table and an invoice line table, you may want to combine elements from both tables into a single query subject called invoices.
- Renaming elements; for example, if you have a column called "City" in many different tables, it will be better to rename the column so that it is related to the corresponding data.
- Assigning standard names and business names to database columns; for example, you may have a database column ORDDATE, which is better to be renamed as Order Date so that it will be understood more easily by the report authors.
- Making use of folders to group similar items.
- Arranging query subject items in a more user-friendly manner.

Sometimes it can be useful to arrange the contents of folders alphabetically, and this can be achieved by using the `Reorder` command for this purpose.

Right-click on the namespace or on the folder to be reordered, and from the pop-up menu select **Reorder**.

- Adding calculations, filters, and prompts.
- Assigning output formats and usages to the reporting elements.

If you create a small folder containing simple items with formats, then they can easily be copied to target items by multiselecting and dragging the item's format through the list.

Presentation layer

The presentation layer is what the report author sees when the published package is used to create reports.

This layer usually only includes shortcuts to the existing items in the logical layer, plus organization items such as folders and namespaces.

For organizing major groupings, you can either use folders or namespaces. However, namespace names must be unique, and items within a namespace must likewise be unique.

If you use folders for your major groupings, then you cannot have similarly named shortcuts in more than one folder.

It is likely that many of the commonly used query subjects will occur in more than one folder, and this can be easily achieved by creating shortcuts to the items and renaming them within the individual folders used to group the subjects.

Dimensional layer

The dimensional layer is required only for models which include Dimensionally Modeled Relation data (DMR) rather than only the relational data.

Specifically, this is for creating regular and measure dimensional query subjects. Much like the presentation layer, this layer is also built upon the logical layer.

This layer is usually created from items in the modeling layer, and can be used to replace the presentation layer if this layer is not required by your report authors.

If there is a dimensional layer in the model, it is usual to include the presentation layer since report authors can then have objects from both layers, which can be combined in the reports.

How to create namespaces

In the Framework Manager, a namespace is a method for grouping objects based on their functionality, for example, for creating the layers of our model. When you create a namespace and publish your package, the items used by the report authors will be prefixed by the name of the namespace. You can have namespaces within namespaces, and each namespace name will have prefix items within the namespace.

The following are the steps to create a namespace:

1. Select the location where the namespace is to be created.
2. Right-click on the **Options** menu and select **Create | Namespace**:

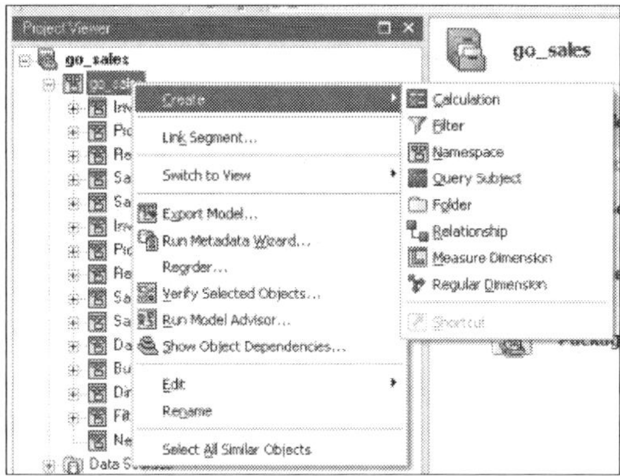

   Alternatively, from the menu select **Create | Namespace**.

3. Give your namespace a name to replace the default name, Namespace. All the names within the model must be unique.

After creating your namespace, you may drag-and-drop the objects into it.

How to create folders

When you publish your package containing folders, the folders are visible to the report authors but unlike namespaces, they are not prefixed to the reporting items.

Unlike namespaces, the folder names are also not prefixed to the items within the folder.

The folders are also created in a similar way to the namespaces:

1. Select the location where the folder is to be created.
2. Right-click on the **Options** menu and select **Create | Folder**.
   Alternatively, from the menu select **Create | Folder**.

3. Give your folder a name to replace the default name. All folder names must be unique within a namespace.
4. You can select and move the objects into the folder, or alternatively click on the **Finish** button to confirm the folder creation.

After creating your folder, you can drag-and-drop other objects into it.

Using the Model Advisor

While creating your framework model, the Model Advisor can be used to verify whether your model follows the current best practice in modeling and also helps to identify those areas of the model that you need to examine and change.

The Model Advisor is not a replacement for an experienced modeler and it should be seen only as a diagnostic tool to assist and improve the model design.

You can run the Model Advisor against the whole model or a subset of the model, and you may also choose which tests should be run against your model.

[Before using the Model Advisor you should verify the model and fix any errors.]

If you are analyzing a newly created model, consider the following points:

- Analyze any newly imported objects, especially their relationships and determinants
- As you import additional database objects and add new relationships and determinants to your model, use the Model Advisor to analyze each change for potential issues
- Before you publish your model for the first time, use the Model Advisor to check all the objects that will be included in your package

If you are analyzing an existing model or a new model that is not yet complete, use the Model Advisor as a tool to validate your modeling practices.

[Model Advisor is intended for use only with relationally based metadata models.

Do not run the Model Advisor against your entire model especially if your model is very large; instead apply it to specific views one at a time.]

How to use the Model Advisor

The Model Advisor is simple to use with the following steps:

1. Select the object to analyze within the model—this would usually be one of the namespaces within the model or a folder within the model.
2. From the **Menu** bar, select **Tools | Run Model Advisor**.

> You can also right-click on one or more objects and then select **Run Model Advisor** from the pop-up menu.
>
> If you selected a namespace and the selected namespace contains additional namespaces or folders, you will see a warning. Click on the **Yes** button to continue.

3. In the **Options** tab, select the items to analyse (an overview of the main options follows this section):

> It is usually better to leave all options selected until you are more familiar with the analysis results.

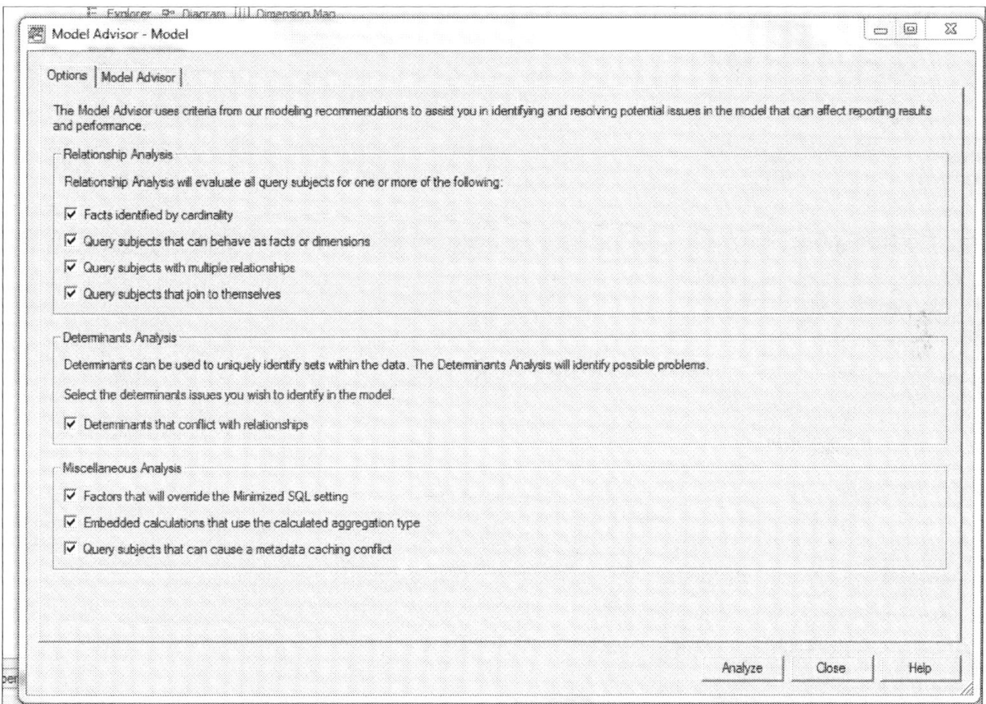

4. Click on the **Analyze** button at the lower right corner of screen to start the analysis.
5. When the analysis has been completed, the results will be shown in the **Model Advisor** tab as follows:

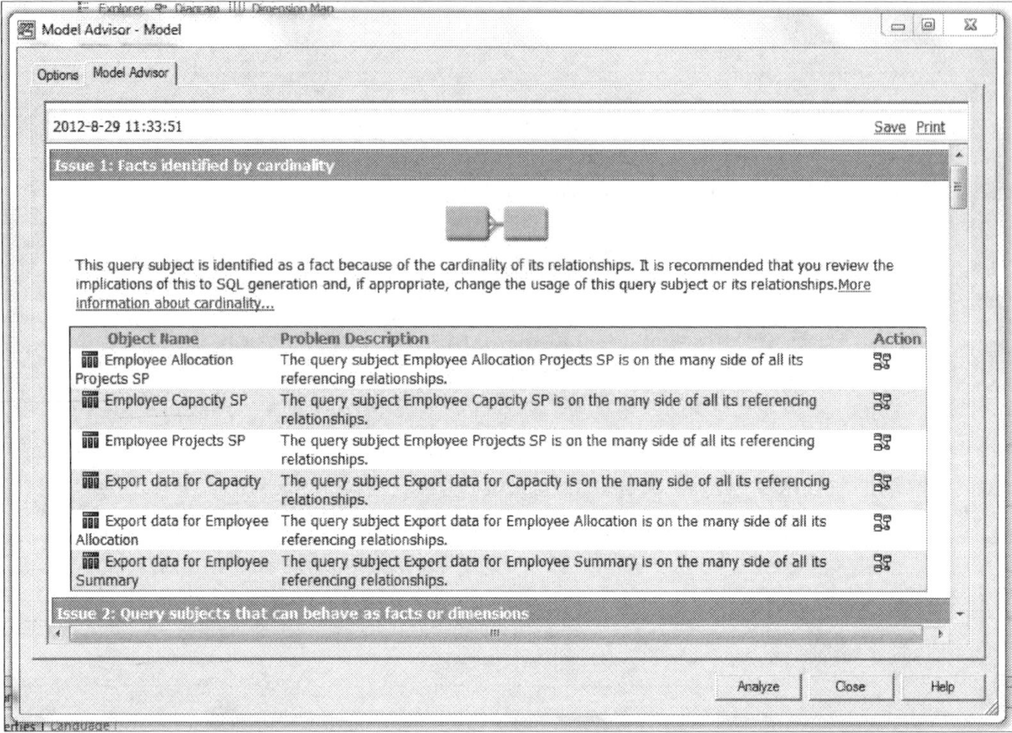

You should review the analysis results carefully since not all items flagged by the Model Advisor indicate a serious problem. Some items may be ignored since they are only warnings about potential problems, while others require fixing so that they do not cause any problems during reporting. The context of any issue flagged by the Model Advisor is important as it helps in determining if the issue indicated needs to be fixed or can be safely ignored.

Facts identified by cardinality

This test looks for query subjects that only have the many (n) cardinality at the end of any relationship in which they are involved. Query subjects with this cardinality will be treated as facts when generating queries, so it is important to ensure that they are correctly identified.

These types of errors may be safely ignored. Sometimes it is necessary to resolve these errors and this can be achieved by setting the cardinality to one (1) instead of many. The only time this needs to be done, however, is when the query subject contains numeric items that have been identified as facts, since they will automatically be included into aggregate functions when used for reporting.

Query subjects that can behave as facts or dimensions

This test looks for query subjects that have many (n) cardinality in relationships to some query subjects and zero or one (0,1) cardinality in relationships to other query subjects. This mixed cardinality means that the query subject can act as both a fact and a dimension depending on other query subjects in the query being generated. If the query subject acts as a fact, it will be included and if it acts as a dimension, it may be skipped, if no items in the query subject are included in the report query.

These types of errors need to be resolved, and this is usually achieved by replacing the cardinalities between the query subject and other query subjects so they are consistent.

Query subjects with multiple relationships

This test looks for query subjects that have multiple relationships between two objects.

If your model has multiple relationships with no distinguishing criteria to choose from, the reporting tools will use the relationship that comes first alphabetically. If you need to create a query that uses a different relationship, you will always have a problem. These types of errors need to be corrected.

To correct the problem associated with multiple relationships, you need to create aliases for the concerned tables and create joins between the original table and the alias tables. For more information on this subject see *Chapter 4, Modeling Relational Data*.

Query subjects that join to themselves

This test looks for reflexive and recursive relationships. Framework Manager will import reflexive relationships but does not use them when executing queries. The usual method for resolving this situation is to transform the data to a flat structure with a fixed number of columns before importing into Framework Manager. For more information on this subject see *Chapter 4, Modeling Relational Data*.

Determinants that conflict with relationships

This test looks for determinants that conflict with the relationship defined for the query subject. Determinants are used to ensure that the aggregation in reports is correct and that queries are generated correctly.

The Model Advisor flags occurrences where the keys of a relationship do not match the keys of a group by determinant.

Problems with determinants need to be resolved to prevent problems with incorrect aggregation in reports.

For more details on determinants see *Chapter 4, Modeling Relational Data*.

Factors that will override the Minimized SQL setting

This test looks out for various factors that override the SQL Generation type setting of Minimized. This usually happens when you have modified data source query subjects, relationships between model query subjects, or determinants for query subjects.

When you use minimized SQL, the generated SQL contains only the minimal set of tables and joins needed to obtain values for the selected query items.

This is an informational message and does not need to be corrected.

Embedded calculations that use the calculated aggregation type

This test detects where you have set the Regular Aggregate property to "calculated" for embedded calculations.

The calculated aggregation type is supported only for the standalone calculations and calculations that are embedded within measure dimensions. This is an informational message rather than an error and does not need to be corrected.

Query subjects that can cause a metadata caching conflict

This test looks for factors that override cached metadata, such as data source query subjects whose SQL has been modified or query subjects that contain calculations or filters.

Framework manager stores the metadata imported from the data source; however this metadata may might not be used when generating a report query if the imported SQL has been modified.

This is an informational message and does not need to be corrected.

Summary

In this chapter, we have looked at some proven practice techniques for improving your modeling with Framework Manager, namely the use of layers to divide your model into functional levels.

We have also looked at the Model Advisor tool, which can be used to diagnose problems with your model, so that if necessary they can be corrected before your model is published.

In the next chapter, we will look at how to import the relational metadata into your new Framework Manager project.

3

Importing Data Sources

This chapter covers the different types of data sources that the Framework Manager can import, and how to import those data sources. This includes the importing of stored procedures, which are an important component of many relational databases. This chapter also includes details on importing OLAP data sources, which do not require modeling but must be imported and then published to make them available to the BI Reporting Studios.

The topics covered in this chapter include:

- Importing metadata from relational data sources
- Using stored procedures as a source of metadata for relational data sources
- Importing from multiple data sources
- Importing metadata from OLAP data sources

By the end of the chapter, you will know how to import data sources into your project.

These imported data sources will form the data layer of your Framework Manager project.

Most Framework projects will start with a relational data source irrespective of whether this is a database, XML, or Excel; they are all considered to be relational data sources. There are also a few exceptions to this, but these tend to be for more specialized data sources that are maintained outside the Cognos environment, such as SAP or Microsoft Analysis Services Cubes.

Importing relational data

To start the import of your relational database metadata into your Framework Manager project, carry out the following steps:

1. Start the Framework Manager, and choose **Create a new project**:

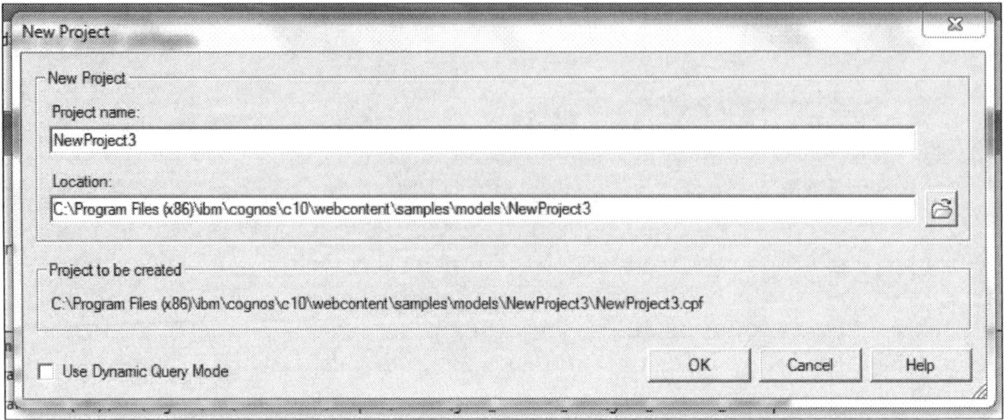

2. Give your project a name, choose the location where the project model will be stored, and then click on the **OK** button.

IBM Cognos now recommends that all new Framework Manager models use the Dynamic Query Mode for all data sources.

3. At the bottom left of this dialog screen, there is a checkbox labeled **Use Dynamic Query Mode**. If you want to turn on the Dynamic Query Mode for your model, then check this box; otherwise leave the box unchecked.

It is not necessary to select Dynamic Query Mode at this stage as it may also be selected later when your package is published.

4. Choose your language for the project, and then click on the **OK** button:

5. Choose the metadata source for the project and then click on the **Next >** button:

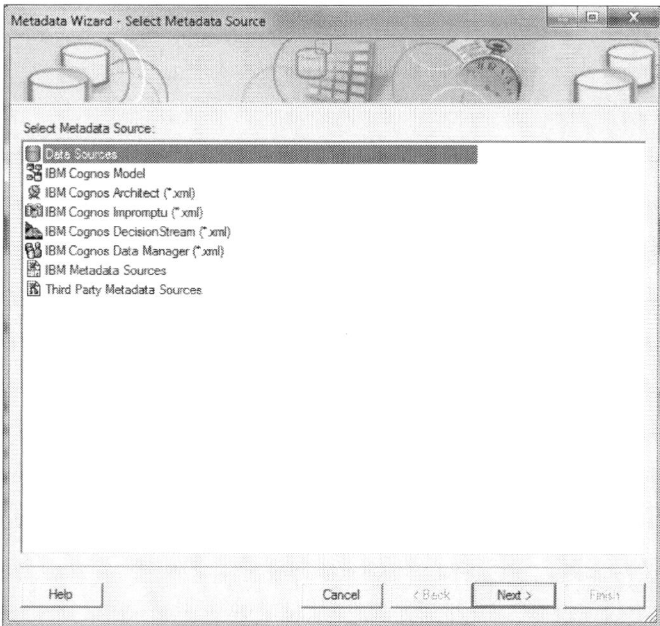

6. By default, the Framework Manager will choose **Data Sources**, which will be highlighted for you. There are also several other sources available:
    - **Data Sources**: This will allow the import of relational data sources. These data sources may be already defined in the Cognos environment, or may be created by the user during the import process.
    - **IBM Cognos Model**: This allows you to import an existing Framework Manager model.
    - **IBM Cognos Architect** and **IBM Cognos Impromptu**: To import metadata from an IBM Cognos Architect model or from an Impromptu catalog, you must first convert it to XML files using the IBM Cognos Migration Assistant.
    - **IBM Cognos DecisionStream** and **IBM Cognos Data Manager**: You can use the IBM Cognos Framework Manager to import metadata from an XML file created by IBM Cognos DecisionStream or IBM Cognos Data Manager.
    - **IBM Metadata Sources**: You can use the IBM Cognos Framework Manager to import metadata from IBM data sources such as IBM InfoSphere DataStage.
7. Accept the **Data Sources** option.
8. You will now be presented with already defined data sources, and a **New** option to create a new data source:

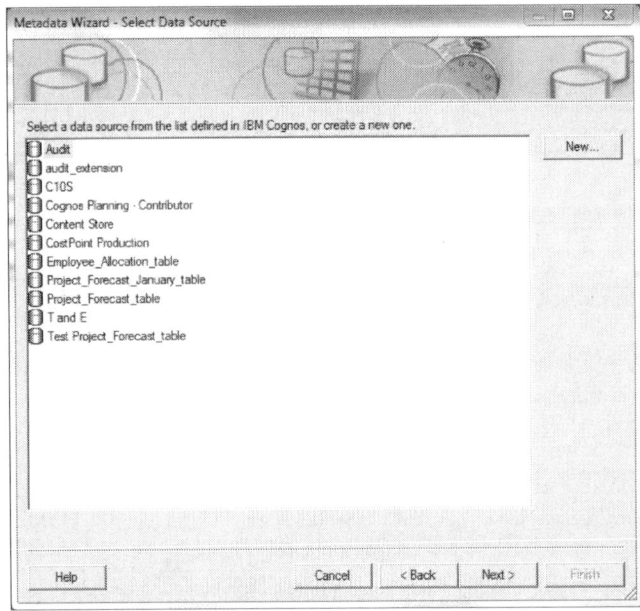

Importing from an existing data source

To start importing from an existing data source, perform the following steps:

1. To use an existing data source, select the data source name and click on the **Next** button.
2. You will now be presented with a tree view of the chosen data source from which the objects can be selected:

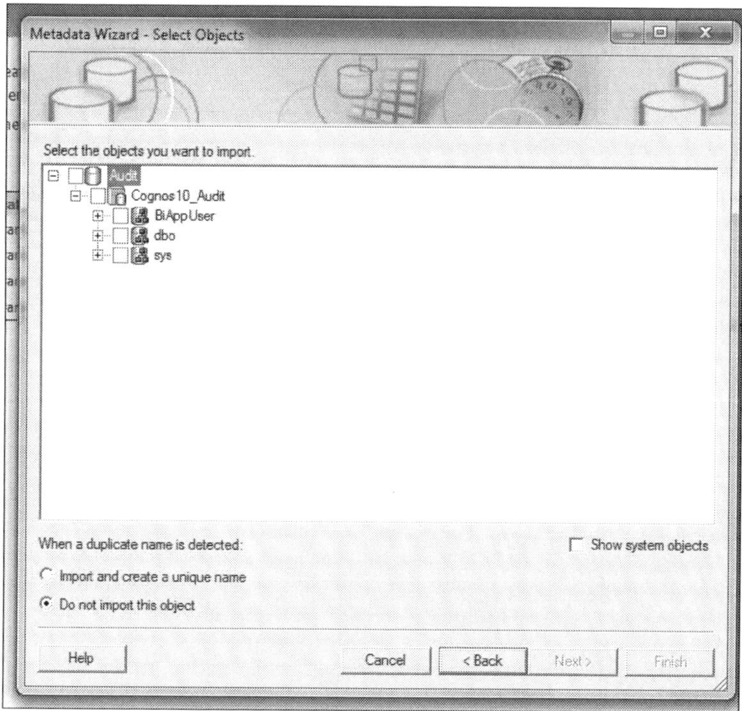

3. Expand the tree view by clicking on the **+** sign besides the object of your choice:

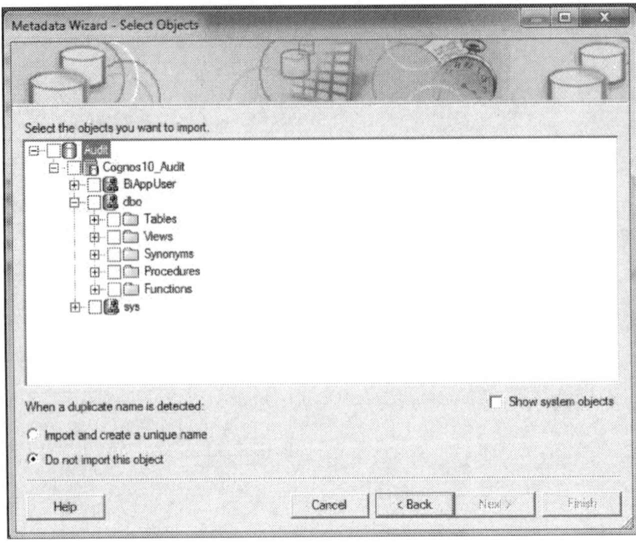

4. As you can see, you have the options to select from **Tables**, **Views**, **Synonyms**, **Procedures**, and **Functions**.
5. You may also expand the tree even further to see more details of your chosen objects:

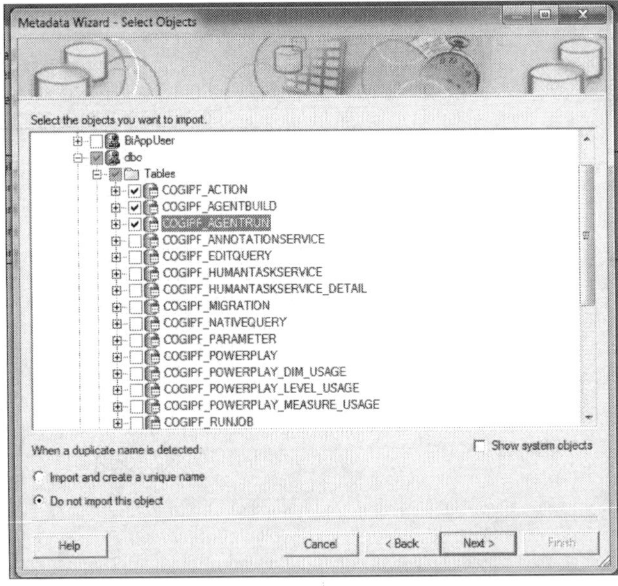

6. Select the objects to be imported by placing a **check** mark into the check box besides the object.

[With a new project only import those database tables that you need initially. If you have several thousand database tables, there is no point in importing them all, if you only use a few.]

7. When you have chosen all the objects to import, click on the **Next** button to import the objects. You will be presented with the options to create relationships between your imported objects:

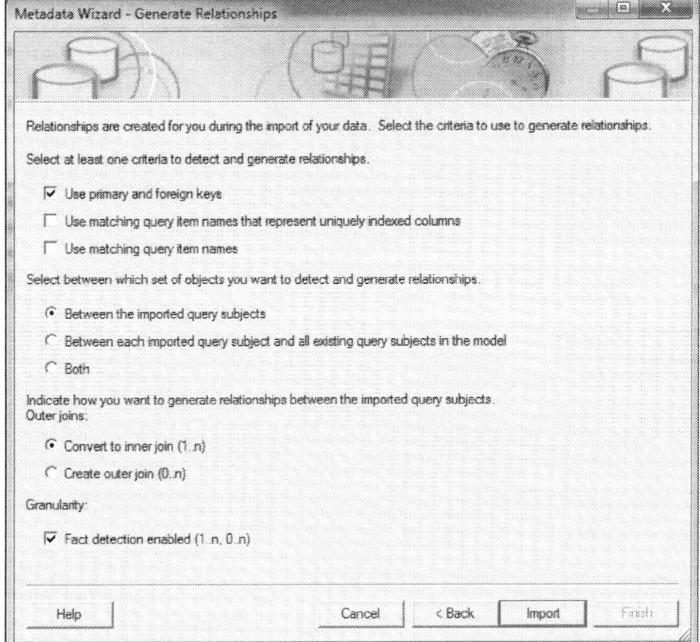

[When allowing the Metadata Wizard to create relationships, do not check the **Use matching query item names** box since this can have unexpected results, if all your tables contain columns called `CreatedDate` or `UpdatedDate`.]

8. When all your selected objects have been imported, you will be presented with a summary of the objects imported, including any joins created between the imported tables:

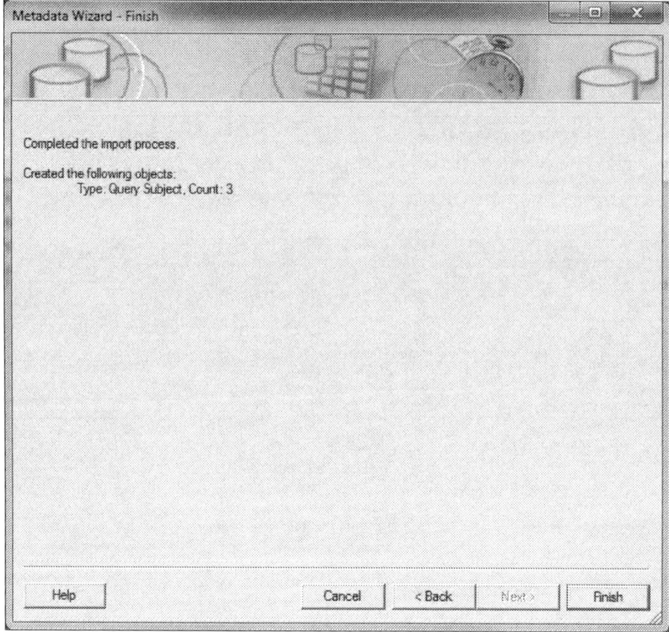

9. Click on the **Finish** button to complete the import process.

Importing from a new data source

To start importing from a new data source, perform the following steps:

1. After selecting **New** on the data sources selection screen, you will be presented with the **New Data Source wizard** screen:

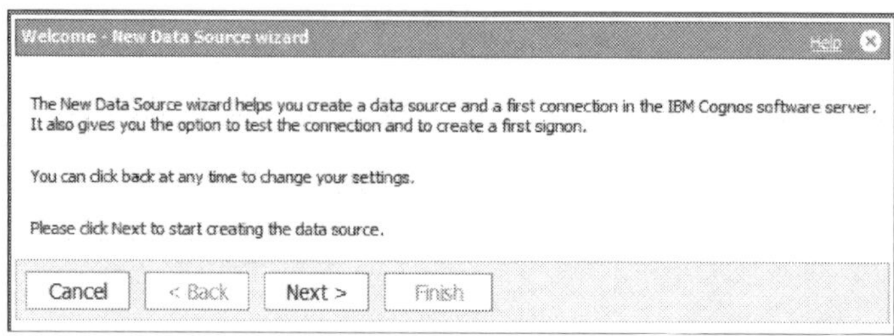

You can also create your new data sources from the Cognos Connection Administrator screens, which uses the same **New Data Source wizard**.

2. Click on the **Next** button to continue:

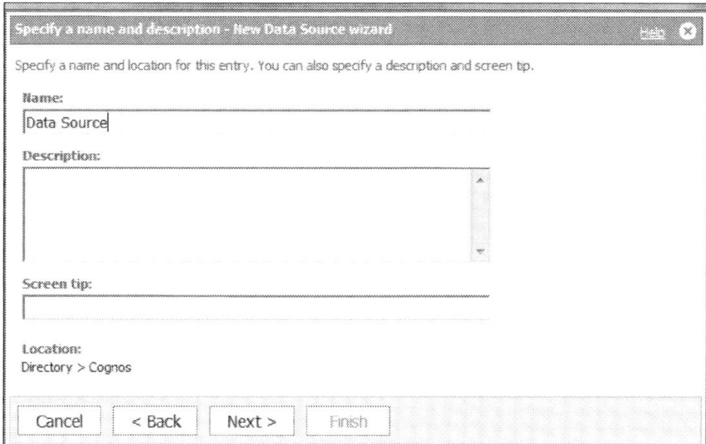

3. Specify a meaningful name and if desired, a description and screen tip for the data source, then click on the **Next** button:

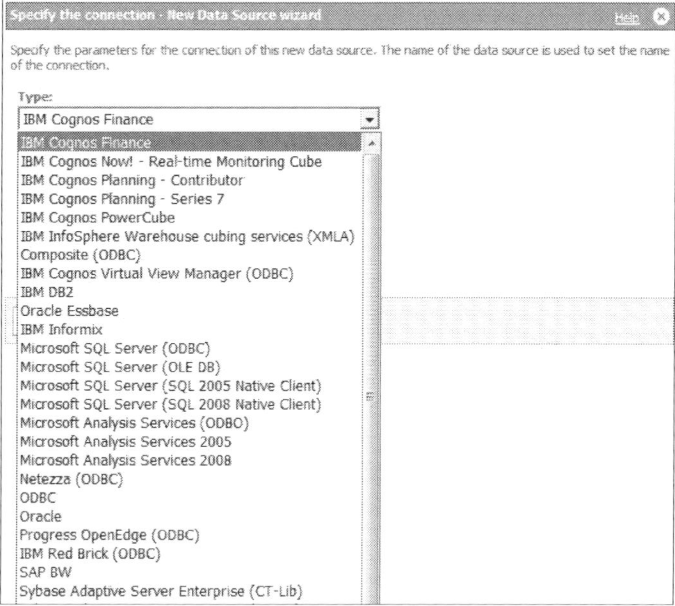

4. From the drop-down box, select the data source type:

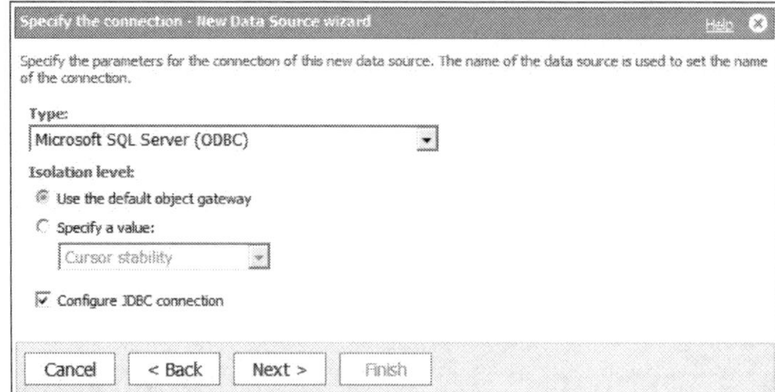

If your data source type is not listed then try ODBC as the data source connection. Most databases will have an ODBC driver available as this is an industry standard.

5. After selecting your data source type, click on the **Next** button to continue.

If you leave the **Configure JDBC connection** box checked, then you will need to provide the JDBC information, which will allow you to use Dynamic Query Mode. If you do not want to provide this information or do not intend to use Dynamic Query Mode then uncheck the box.

Dynamic Query Mode is an enhanced Java based query engine, originally designed for OLAP processing and now also recommended for relational processing. Further details on Dynamic Query Mode can be found in the IBM Cognos documentation and on the IBM Cognos website.

6. Fill in all the information required for your data source connection, and click on the **Next** button to continue.

[Always select **Test the connection** after creating a new connection.]

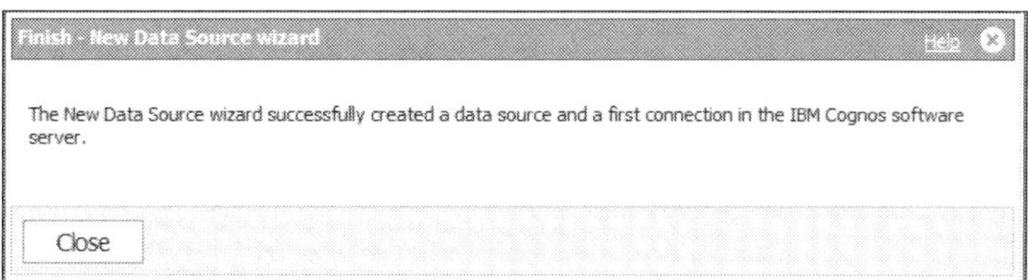

7. When you have finished creating your data source connection, click on the **Close** button. You can now continue to import the metadata for your data source.
8. Follow the same steps described in the *Importing from an existing data source* and *Importing from a new data source* sections to import the data source objects.

Importing stored procedures

When you import your metadata from a relational data source, you can also import stored procedures. The Framework Manager only supports the import of user-defined stored procedures. When you have imported your stored procedure, you can treat it as if it were a database table and can create joins to other objects.

You can import your stored procedures as part of the initial import of metadata or at a later time. After importing your stored procedure into the Framework Manager, the procedure must first be run in order to get a description of the result set that the procedure returns.

There are certain rules that imported stored procedures must follow for them to work with the Framework Manager:

- The stored procedure must return a single result set. The Framework Manager only supports the first result set that is returned.
- If the procedure could conditionally return a different result set, then any result set returned should be in the same form, with the same number, types, and names for the returned columns.
- The output parameters are not supported.

When you have imported a stored procedure, the query will display as a broken object. You must run the stored procedure to validate it and return the underlying query subject definition.

When you update a stored procedure in the data source, running the stored procedure in the Framework Manager will update the query subject using the newly generated query items.

Using prompts with a stored procedure

If your stored procedure has parameters, you can define prompts for your stored procedure variables, and your users can then set the variables in reports.

The following example uses a stored procedure called `Projects_Details`, which has a single parameter `@Project_Id`:

```
DEFINE PROCEDURE Project_Details
  @Project_ID varchar(4)
BEGIN
  .<stored procedure code>
END
```

We perform the following steps for using prompts with a stored procedure:

1. Create a stored procedure query subject that uses the `Projects_Details` stored procedure.
2. The **Query Subject Definition** dialog box displays as follows:

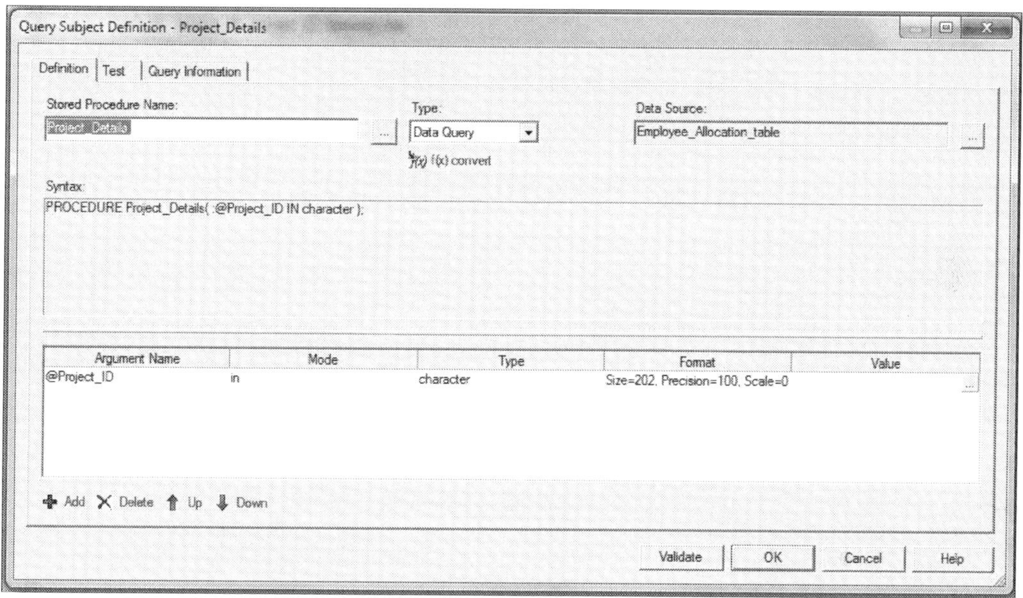

3. In the **Definition** tab, select the **@Project_ID** argument, and click on the ellipsis (**...**) button.
4. In the **Value** box, type the following macro syntax and then click on **OK**:

   `#prompt('Project Id ','text')#`

5. If you want to test the prompt for the variable, perform the following steps:
    1. Click on the **Test** | **Test Sample** option.
    2. The **Prompt Values** dialog box is displayed.

3. In the **Name** column, click on **Project ID**.
4. In the **Value** field, type **1234** and then click on **OK**.
5. One record is returned, showing the data for **Project ID** as **1234**.
6. The Framework Manager uses this value for the duration of the current session or until you clear the prompt value.

6. Click on **OK**.

Importing additional database objects

After completing the initial import of data source objects into your Framework Manager project, it is sometimes necessary to import additional objects into your project.

Importing from the same data source

To import additional tables from your existing data source:

1. Right-click on the namespace where you have already imported your data source:

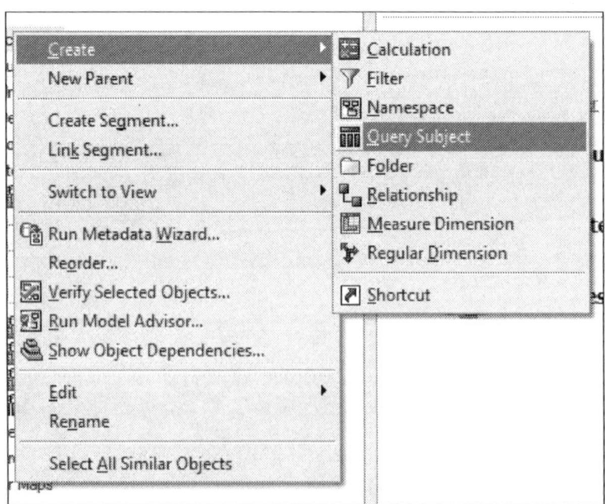

2. Select **Create** | **Query Subject**.

You can also choose **Run Metadata Wizard** to import additional objects from your data source.

These options are also available from **Actions** in the menu bar.

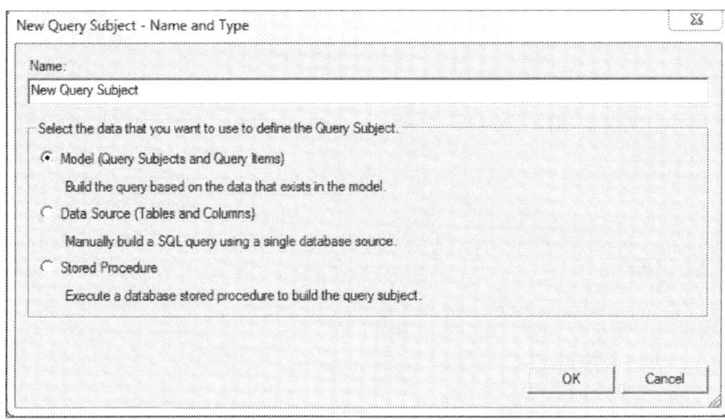

3. Give your Query Subject a name, and ensure that **Data Source (Tables and Columns)** is checked.
4. Follow the same steps as in the *Importing from an existing data source* section.

Importing from additional data sources

It is not necessary for all the objects to be imported from the same database or data source, you may also import objects from many different data sources into the same project.

If you import data from different database sources and join tables from the different databases, then this may impact the performance of your reports since the joins need to be made within the Cognos Server.

To import additional data sources in order to run the Metadata Wizard from the menu bar, choose **Action | Run Metadata Wizard**, or right-click on your project and then choose **Run Metadata Wizard**.

Importing OLAP data sources

Examples of OLAP data sources are IBM Cognos PowerCubes, Microsoft Analysis Services Cubes, SAP BW, and Oracle Essbase. Although they can also act as data sources for Framework Manager, it is not necessary to model them; but it is necessary to create and publish packages for the IBM Cognos reporting tools.

To import your OLAP data source into your Framework Manager project, proceed in the same way as for importing relational data sources, and choose your OLAP data source.

At the end of the import, a summary screen will display telling you that the import process has been completed:

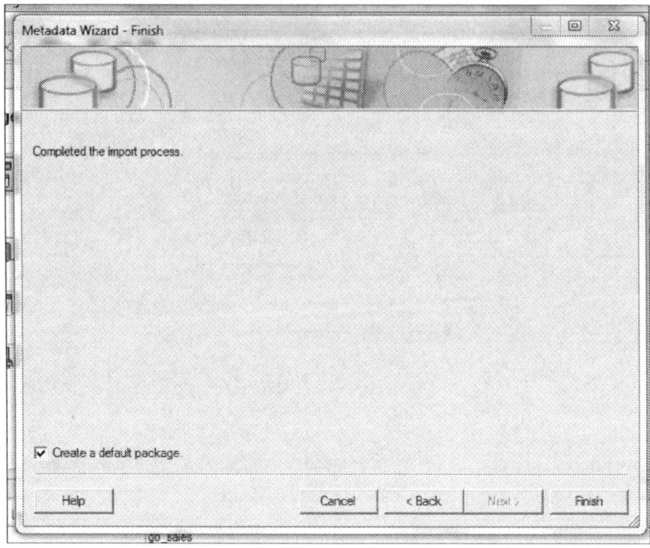

Check the **Create a default package** box, and click on the **Finish** button. You can now specify a name for your package and publish it to your Cognos Server in the usual way.

You do not need to do anything more with your OLAP data source; all the modeling of the data has been done in the data source itself, and you are merely providing a mechanism to make the data source available to your report authors.

Combining OLAP and relational data sources

Although there is no restriction on importing both relational and OLAP data sources into your Framework Manager project, you need to be aware of two things when adding OLAP data sources:

1. The metadata for OLAP sources is checked when the package is opened in one of the BI Studios. If there are a lot of cubes in the package, it will take a long time for the package to open or it may not open at all.

2. If an OLAP source is not available, the package will not open even if the relational sources are available.

Your Report Designers will need to be made aware that there are relational and OLAP data sources available within the published packages since combining data from the different sources may add complexity to the reporting.

After importing your data sources

If you did not import your data sources into the correct layer of your Framework Manager model, then you can drag-and-drop all of you data source objects into the correct layer.

Summary

In this chapter, we have looked into some of the different types of data that can be imported into your project. We have looked into the import of relational data sources since these will be the main data source for many of our projects, and we have also looked into the use of stored procedures as a data source within a relational database. We have briefly mentioned OLAP data sources since they do not require any additional modeling for your project.

To follow the rules established in *Chapter 2, Proven Practice*, we will have to import our data sources into the data layer of our Framework Manager model.

In the next chapter, we will look at modeling our data sources to create the necessary relationship between objects. We will also look at the rules for cardinality and determinants.

4

Modeling Relational Data

After importing the metadata from your relational data source, you must ensure that it meets the reporting requirements of your users. This chapter will cover the modeling of the relationships between the data tables.

The topics covered in this chapter include:

- Dimension and fact tables
- Cardinality
- Determinants
- Role playing dimensions
- Loop joins
- Reflexive and recursive joins

By the end of this chapter, you will have modeled the relationships between the tables in an imported relational data source.

During the import process Framework Manager can automatically create the relationships between tables for you. In this situation it is important to review the created relationships to ensure that they give the correct results for use by the report authors.

Most modelers will choose not to allow the import process to create the relationships between tables. As a result, the modeler must create the relationships themselves.

In creating relationships, Framework Manager uses the data warehouse terminology of dimension tables and fact tables, because there is an inbuilt assumption that the modeler is modeling a data mart or data warehouse. This is not always true in all cases since most modelers will probably be modeling a transactional data processing system.

Two of the most important aspects of creating joins in Framework Manager are cardinality and determinants.

Cardinality

Framework manager uses the cardinality of the joins between tables to identify dimension and fact tables.

Cardinality affects how queries are written, and thus affects the results of the query. Framework Manager allows cardinality to be specified by the modeler or generated based on the criteria while importing from the database.

The general rules that apply to cardinality are as follows:

- Cardinality is applied in the context of a query, and only the cardinalities of items explicitly included in the query are evaluated
- Query subjects defined with one-to-many or zero-to-many cardinalities are always identified as facts
- Query subjects defined with one-to-one or zero-to-one cardinalities are always identified as dimensions
- It is possible to have a query subject that behaves as a dimension in one query and as a fact in another

A query subject that has only maximum (n) cardinality for all of its relationships to other query subjects can be regarded as a fact. This implies that there are always more rows of data in the fact query subject than in the related query subject on the minimum (1) side of the relationship.

A query subject having at least one relationship to another query subject with minimum cardinality (1) will be treated as a dimension.

Detecting cardinality during import

When importing the table definitions from a relational data source, cardinality can be detected based on a set of rules chosen by the modeler as part of the import process.

[If you want to model all the relationships yourself, then ensure that all options are unchecked.]

These rules are can be selected from the following:

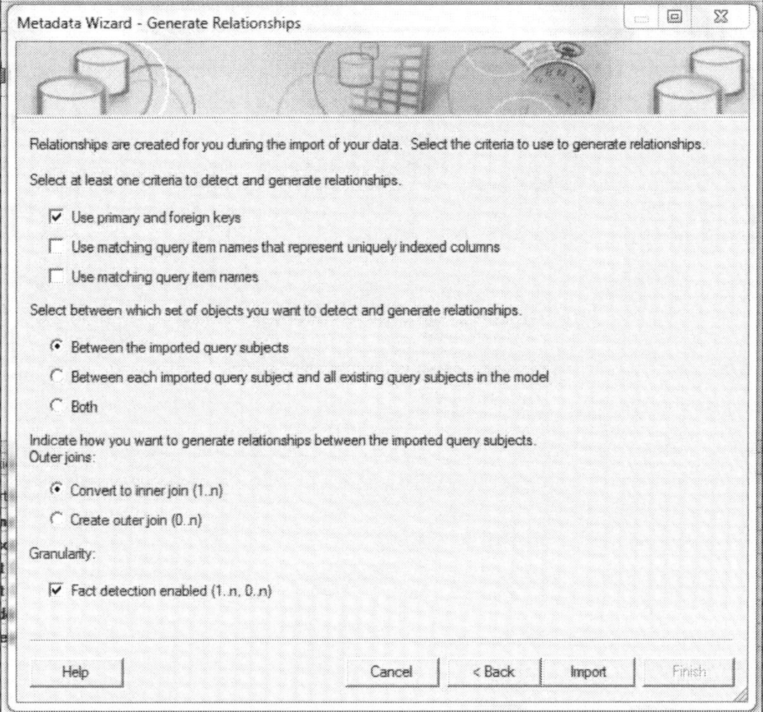

The default option for creating relationships during the import process is to select **Use primary and foreign keys** as these will already be defined in the data source.

Whichever options are used to import your metadata and generate relationships, it is important to remember that you are adding this information to your model.

If you do not want the import process to automatically detect the relationships between tables, then ensure that all options are unchecked before clicking on the **Import** button.

Never select the **Use matching query item names** option, unless you are sure that this is what you really want, as it can have unexpected results.

Creating relationships and cardinality

Most modelers will create relationships between tables themselves. Even after allowing Framework Manager to create the relationships automatically, business demands may require that the modeler creates additional relationships, and amends or removes the automatically generated relationships.

When creating relationships it is best to close the **Tools** pane, keeping the **Project Viewer** and **Properties** windows visible, and change the project pane to show the **Diagram** tab.

To manually create relationships between tables, perform the following steps:

1. Expand the **Project Viewer** window until the tables you want to join are visible.
2. Select the first table by clicking on it, and select the second table by pressing the *Ctrl* key before selecting the table - both the tables will appear in the **Properties** pane:

Be consistent in selecting your tables, because whichever table appears on the left-hand side of the join is determined by the table selected first.

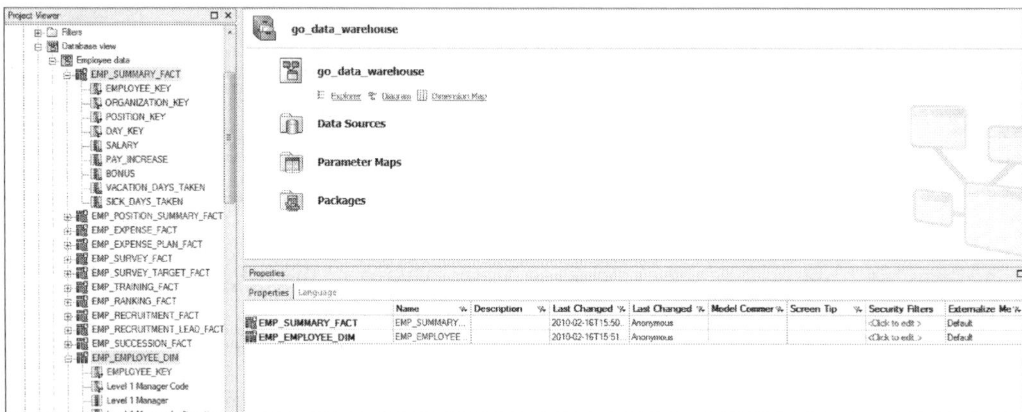

3. Right-click on the table and select **Create Relationship**, or from the **Actions** menu, navigate to **Create | Relationship**:

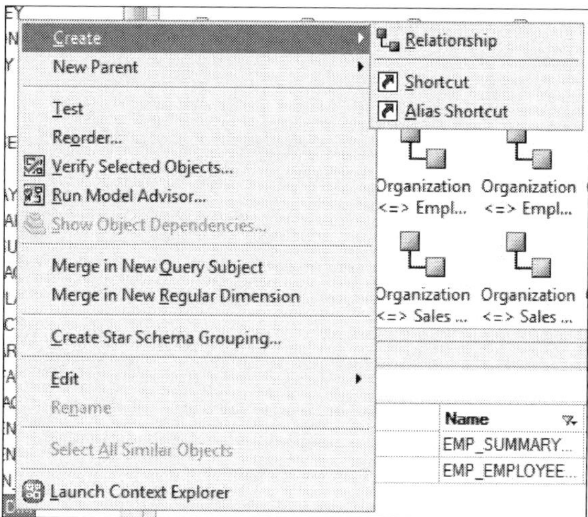

4. Select the columns to be used to create the join between the tables – the selected columns will be highlighted and joined by a line:

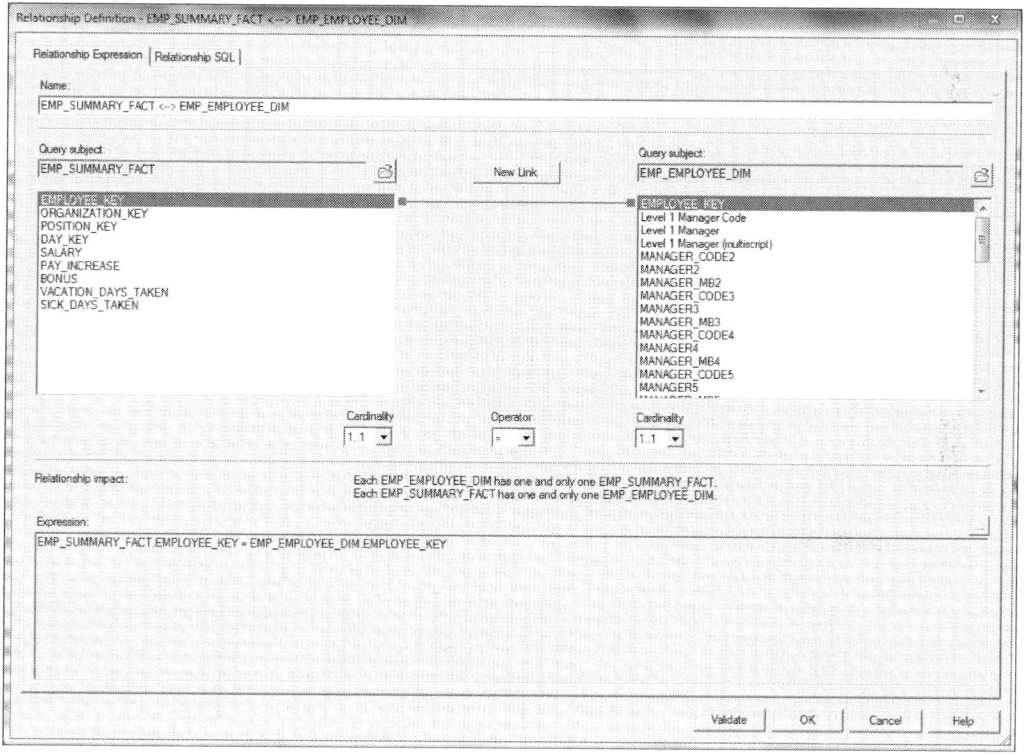

5. To add additional columns click on the **New Link** button, and select the columns to be joined.
6. Set the cardinality on each end of the relationship join.
7. Use the statement in the **Relationship impact** section to verify that you have correctly set the cardinality.

The usual join operator is =, but by clicking on the drop-down box next to the operator label, other operators such as >, <, <=, >=, and <> may be selected. More complex operators may also be selected by clicking on the ellipsis to the right of the statements in the **Relationship impact** section.

8. Use the **Relationship SQL** tab to view the SQL that will be generated by the join just created between the two tables:

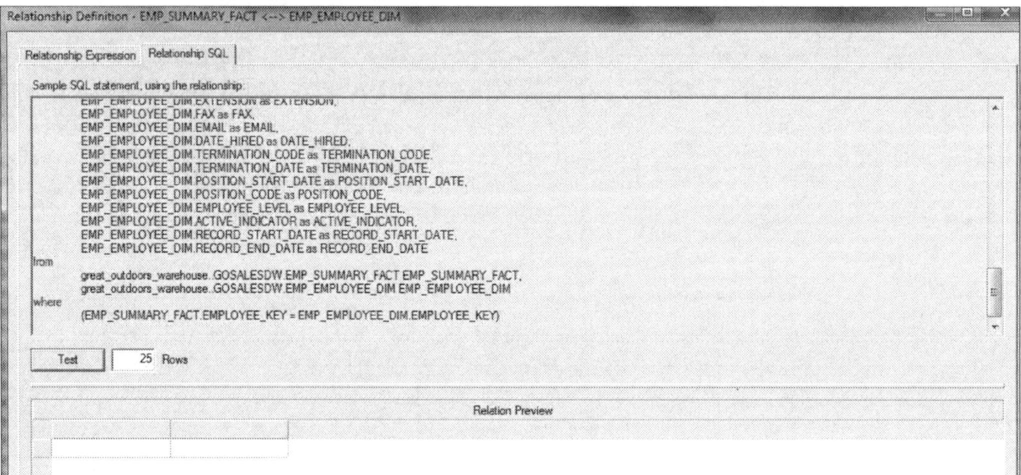

9. The SQL may be tested by clicking on the **Test** button.
10. When the defined relationship is correct, click the **OK** button to confirm the relationship between the selected tables.

To verify or review all the relationships for any table, right-click on the table and select the **Launch Context Explorer** option.

Determinants

Determinants are one of the most confusing aspects of Framework Manager and are therefore the least understood. As a result, many modelers will never use or create them. However, determinants can play an important role in the performance of your Framework Manager model.

Determinants allow a table with one level of detail (or granularity) to behave as if it has a completely different level of detail. Generally determinants will be used with dimension tables, where fact tables join the dimension table at more than one level in the dimension.

A common example of where determinants would be used is with a date dimension table, with a granularity at the day level. If all the fact tables are joined to this table at the day level, there would be no need for determinants.

A join between a monthly forecast table aggregated at the month level with one row per month, and with this date dimension table would return between 28 and 31 records, depending upon the month. This could cause problems when applying the aggregate functions such as `sum()` or `count()` to the result. In this case, using determinants will solve this problem.

If we create a report only from the monthly forecast fact table, we will see the following details in our report:

Month_Id	Forecast_Value
1	200
2	300

Now if we add a column from the date dimension table, we will see the following details in our report:

month_name	Month_Id	Forecast_Value
January	1	6,200
February	2	8,400

This is obviously not reporting the correct values, since the value for January is being multiplied by 31, and for February by 28. We can correct this situation by adding determinants to the date dimension, and we will now see the correct value in our report:

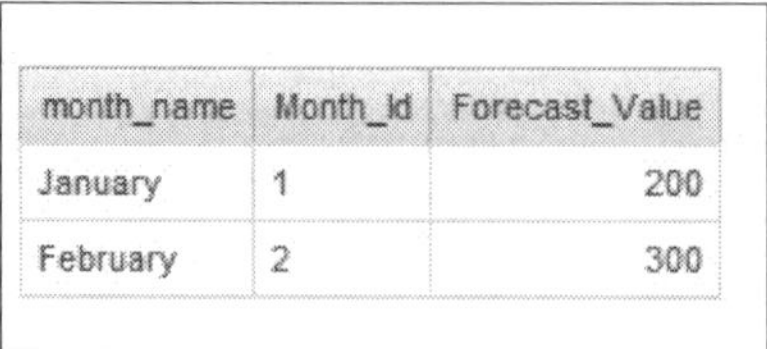

month_name	Month_id	Forecast_Value
January	1	200
February	2	300

If we examine the SQL generated by Report Studio, we can see the effects of the determinants.

We see the following SQL without determinants:

```
SELECT date_dimension.month_name AS "month_name",
       Sum(monthly_forecast_fact.forecast_value) AS "Forecast_Value"
FROM   date_dimension date_dimension
       INNER JOIN monthly_forecast_fact          monthly_forecast_fact
               ON date_dimension.month_number = monthly_forecast_fact.
month_id
GROUP  BY date_dimension.month_name
```

We see the following SQL with determinants:

```
SELECT date_dimension3.month_name                AS "month_name",
       Sum(monthly_forecast_fact.forecast_value) AS "Forecast_Value"
FROM   (SELECT date_dimension.month_number       AS "month_number",
               Min(date_dimension.month_name)    AS "month_name"
        FROM   date_dimension date_dimension
        GROUP  BY date_dimension.month_number)      date_dimension3
       INNER JOIN monthly_forecast_fact             monthly_forecast_
fact
               ON date_dimension3.month_number = monthly_forecast_
fact.month_id
GROUP  BY date_dimension3.month_name
```

How to add determinants

If we look at the date dimension table, there are four possible determinants that we can add to the table, such as year, quarter, month, and day. We are only interested in the month level at this stage so we will create a determinant for the month as follows:

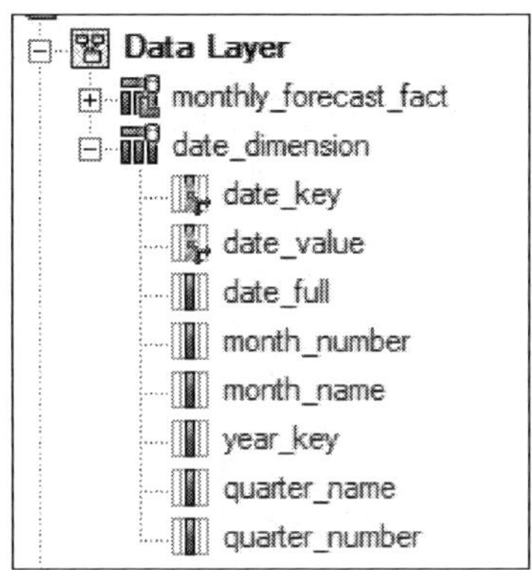

The table has a primary key called **date_key**. If we allowed the import process to create relationships then it will also create determinants using this key.

We add determinants as follows:

1. Right-click on the **Query**, and from the pop-up menu choose **Edit Definition**, or navigate to **Query | Edit Definition** from the **Actions** menu.
2. Select the **Determinants** tab:

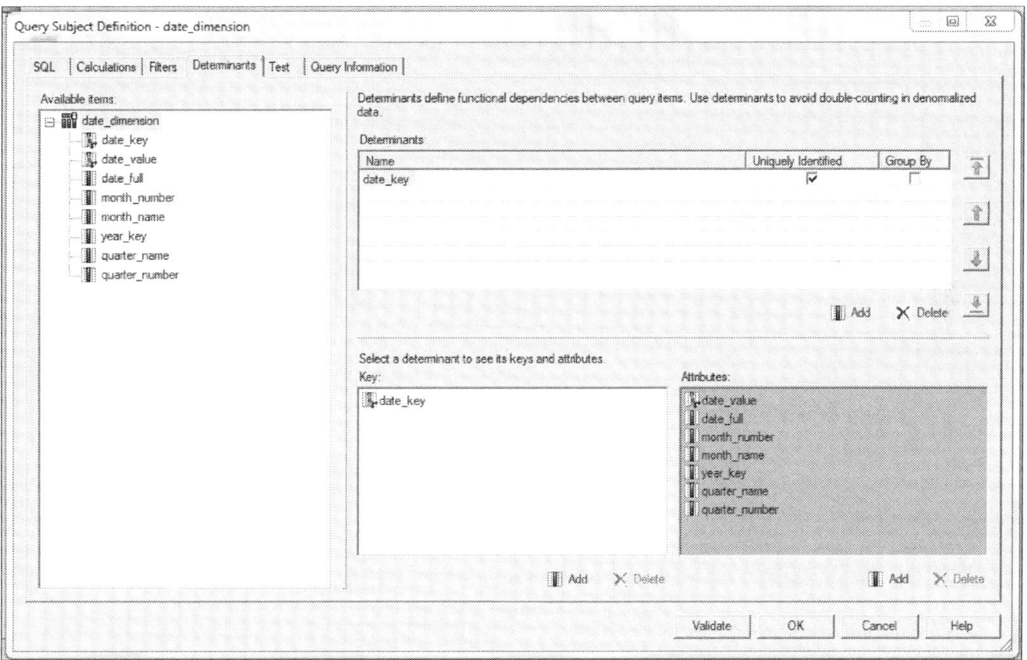

We can see the **date_key** determinant is declared as **Uniquely Identified**, since this is the primary key on the table and we will keep this determinant.

3. Click on the **Add** label below the **Determinants** panel, and this will add our new determinant.

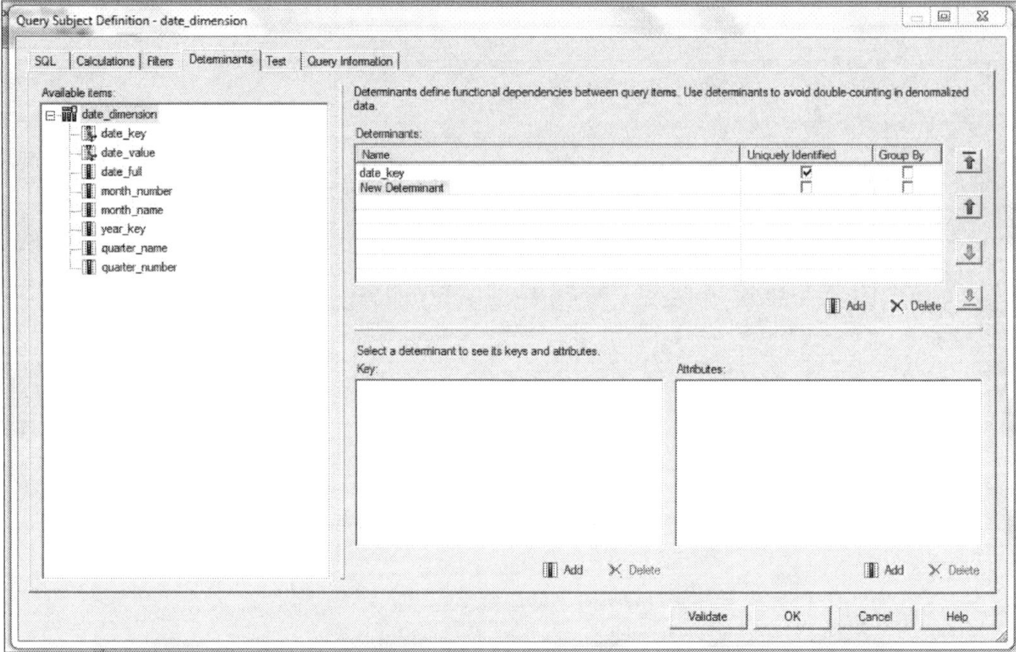

4. Click on the **New Determinant** label, and then press the *F2* key to rename the determinant as **Month**.
5. Select the **Group By** check box besides this label.
6. Drag-and-drop **month_number** from the **Available items** panel into the **Key** panel, or select **month_number** from the **Available items** panel, and click on the **Add** label below the **Key** panel.
7. Drag-and-drop all the other available items into the **Attributes** panel, or select each item in turn and then click on the **Add** label below the Attributes panel.

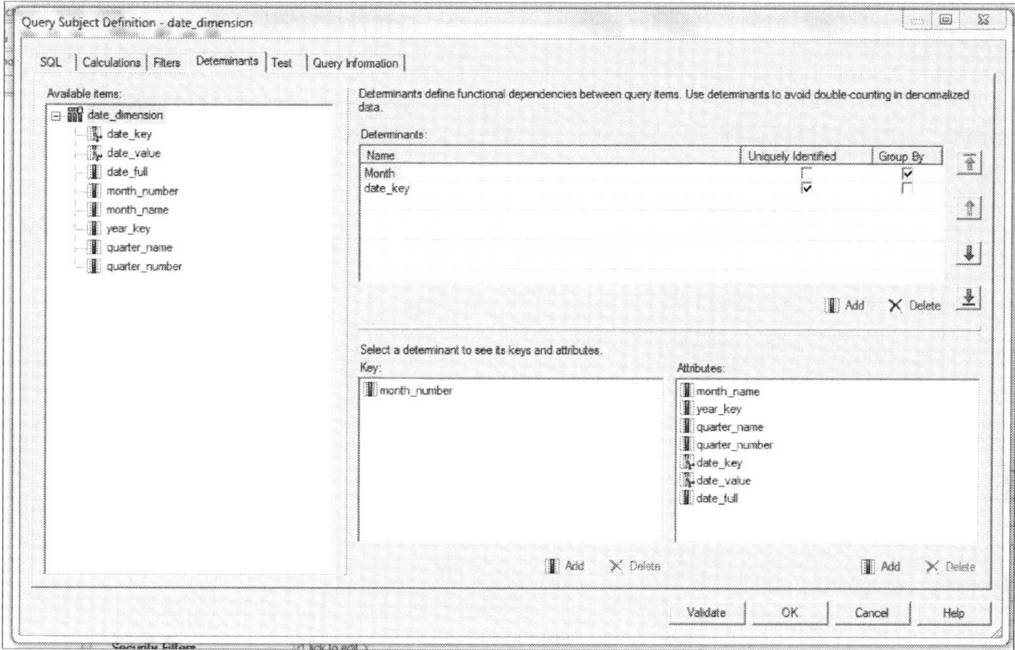

8. Reorder the determinants so that they are in "top-down" order. Use the up and down arrow buttons at the right of the **Determinants** panel to do this.
9. Click on **OK** to confirm the changes.

To check that the determinant has been correctly created, you will need to publish the package containing the tables and create a report with Report Studio.

Special purpose joins

There are some special purpose joins which cannot be automatically generated during the import of the data source from your relational database. These special purpose joins can only by created by the modeler.

Role playing dimensions

A table that has multiple relationships between itself and another table is known as a role playing dimension. A good example is an Orders Fact, which may have multiple relationships to the Customer Dimension on keys such as Sold To, Ship To, and Bill To:

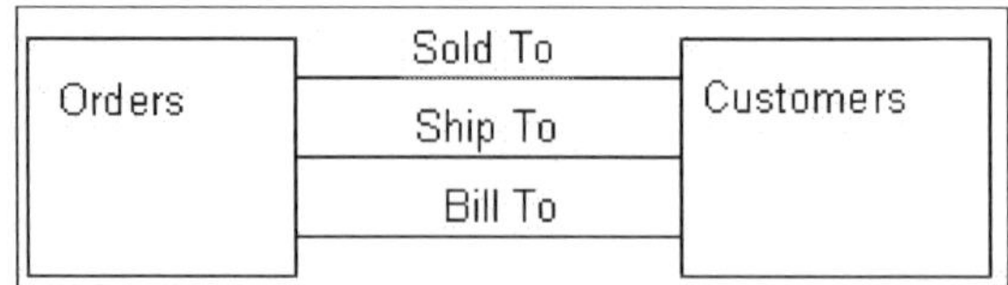

This situation can create problems with joins in Framework Manager since there are now multiple joins paths between two tables. If you run the Model Advisor (see *Chapter 2, Proven Practice*), this is one of the of the errors which will be diagnosed and must be fixed in the model.

The solution in Framework Manager is to create a model query subject for each role. The model query subjects query items that can then be renamed to have an appropriate name for their use. A single relationship can then be created between each model query subject and the fact query subject:

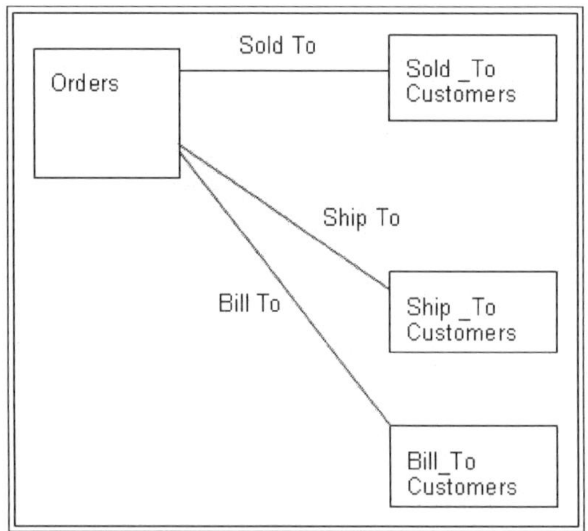

Reflexive and recursive joins

This is the second type of special purpose join which has to be created by the modeler. A reflexive or recursive join is simply a table which joins back to itself. This type of structure is often used to create a hierarchy in a single database table.

Framework Manager will import recursive relationships but cannot use them when executing queries. To create a functioning recursive relationship, you must create a shortcut to the query subject or model query subjects based on the query subject (an alias) and then create a relationship between the query subject and the alias. This would have to be repeated for each level you wish to represent.

For a simple two-level structure, the model would look as follows:

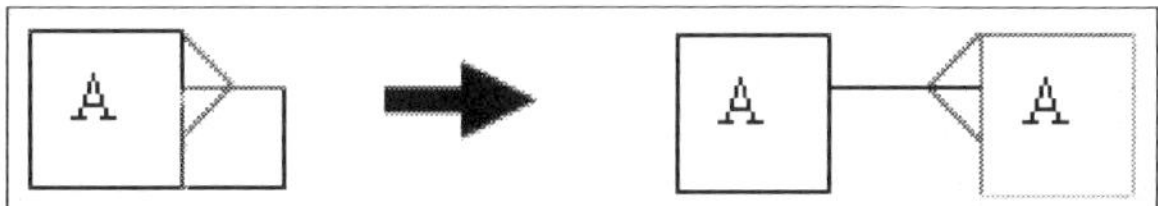

For each additional level it would be necessary to create another alias and join it appropriately:

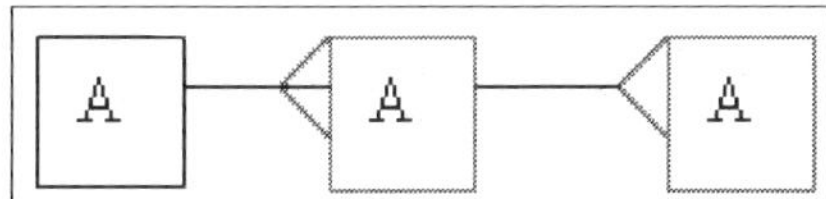

Using a model query subject is often a more attractive option because you can specify which query items are included in the query subject.

[When dealing with a deeply recursive hierarchy, the hierarchy should be flattened in the database and the resulting flattened table (or view) should then be modeled as a single query subject.]

Where to model the relationships

It is important to model the relationships and set determinants on the objects in the Framework Manager model, but an important consideration is where this modeling should take place.

If you allow Framework Manager to create the relationships for you during the import process then the relationships will be created in the Import (or Database) layer of the model. If you create the relationships or add determinants manually, then you are free to create them in any layer of the model. However, best practice dictates that they should be in the Import or Database layer of the model.

[Wherever you create your relationships and add determinants, do this only in one layer of the model.]

Summary

In this chapter, we have learned how to model relational data in Framework Manager. We have learned how to create relationships, and add determinants to the model.

We now have an understanding of the effects of cardinality on determining whether a table is a fact or a dimension table. We have looked at how determinants can affect the way data is aggregated.

We have learned how to model some special relationships which cannot be created by the data import process.

In the next chapter, we will look at modeling dimensionally modeled relational data in Framework Manager.

5
Modeling Dimensional Data

This chapter will cover the use of dimensional modeling, which is more correctly called **Dimensionally Modeled Relational (DMR)** data. The dimensional models created can be used with IBM Cognos Analysis Studio, and also with the other studios.

In this chapter we will cover the following:

- Creating regular dimensions
- Creating regular dimensions with multiple hierarchies
- Creating measure dimensions
- Creating scope dimensions

By the end of this chapter, you will be able to create a dimensional data model using relational data sources.

Dimensional modeling is the name for a set of techniques and concepts used in data warehouse design. Dimensional modeling is based on the concepts of dimensions (or context) and facts (or measures). Dimensions are groups of hierarchies and descriptors that define the facts; facts are typically numeric values that can be aggregated.

Dimension modeling is one of the functions available within Framework Manager. With the dimensional modeling capability you can create dimensions with hierarchies at different levels, and facts with multiple measures. You can then create a scope relationship between the measures and facts.

DMR packages can be used in Analysis Studio, Query Studio, and Report Studio. They enable drilling up and drilling down within the reports, and give access to the member functions within the Report Studio.

The data layer forms the basis for modeling your dimensional data.

You do not create joins between your dimensions and facts. Instead you create the joins on the query subjects in the data layer and then create a scope relationship between the dimensions and the facts.

[Following the principles of proven practice, create your dimensions in a separate dimensional layer of your model.]

Regular dimensions

A regular dimension contains one or more user-defined hierarchies, with each hierarchy consisting of the following components:

- **Levels**: These are used to roll-up measures
- **Keys**: Each item in a level must have a unique key defined
- **Captions**: These are used as labels for the levels
- **Attributes**: These contain additional information regarding the levels

Every regular dimension requires that each level has a key and a caption specified, and that the caption be a string data type.

Regular dimensions are based on data source or model query subjects that have already been defined in your model.

Creating a regular dimension

We will create a time dimension using the great_outdoors_warehouse from the IBM Cognos Samples. From the model, we will use the Time query from the Business view item as a relational data source to build our regular dimension.

Create your regular dimension as follows:

1. Right-click on your namespace, and navigate to **Create** | **Regular Dimension**, or alternatively click on your namespace and from the **Actions** menu, navigate to **Create** | **Regular Dimension**. This will show the dimension definition dialog box as follows:

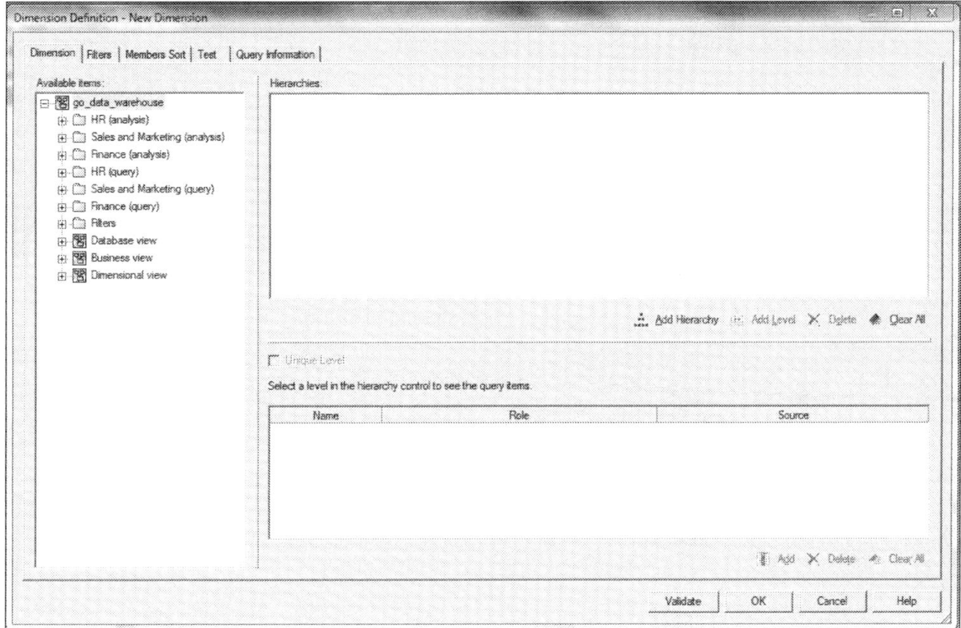

2. Expand the **Business view** item to locate and expand the **Time** query:

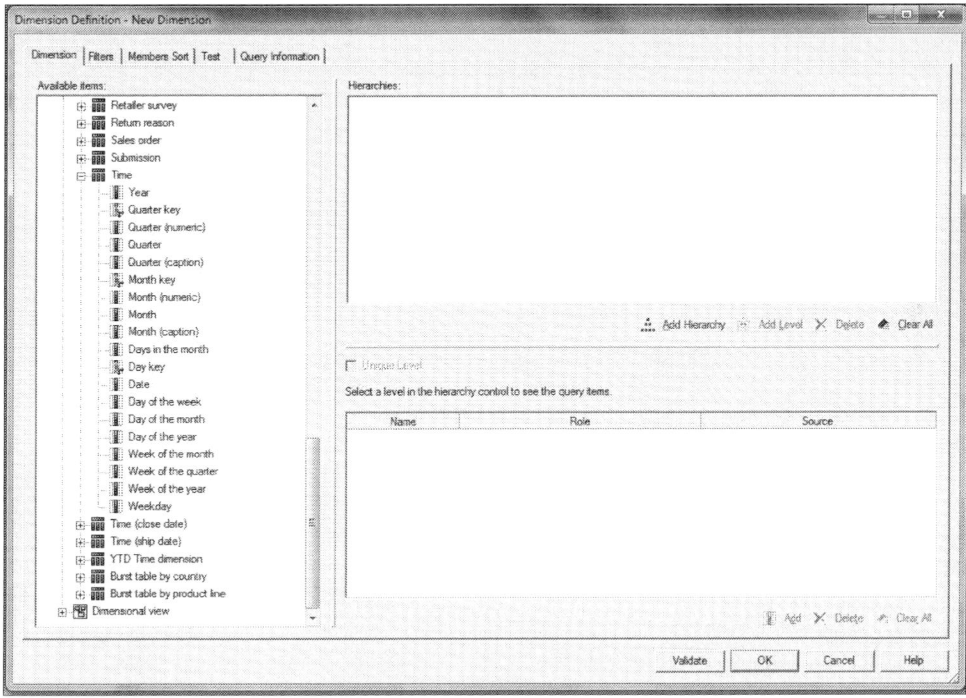

3. Drag-and-drop the **Year** item from the **Available items** into the **Hierarchies** panel:

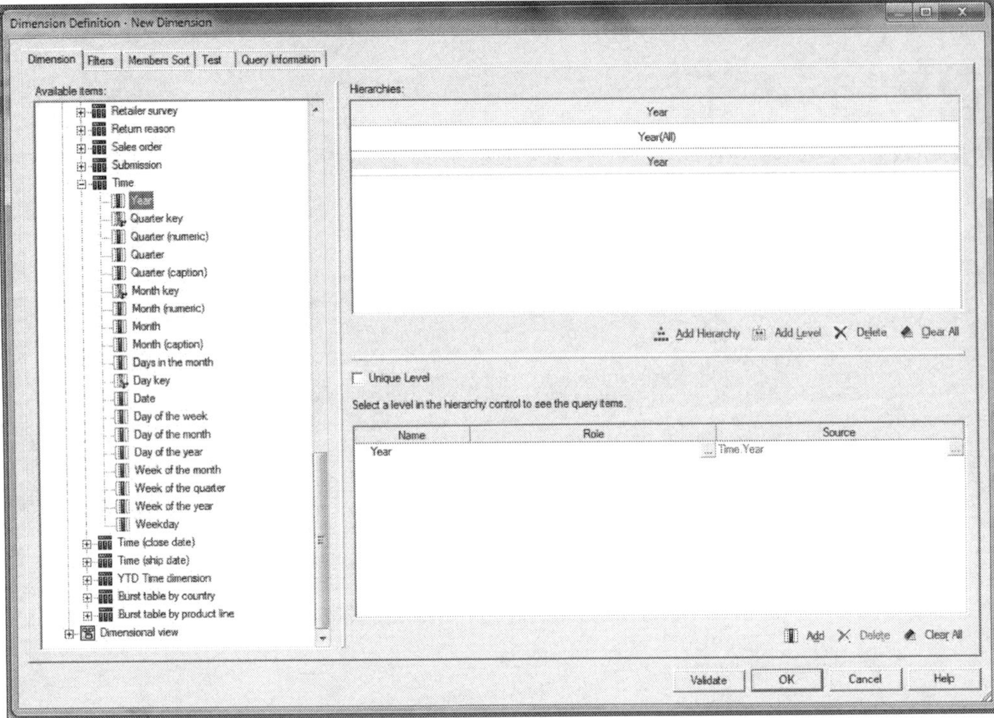

4. In the lower-right panel under the **Role** heading click on the ellipsis (**...**) button, and from the pop-up screen select **_businessKey** (a key which is used to identify the record), and **_memberCaption** (this is simply a label to display when the item is used), and then click on the **Close** button.

[`Year` is a numeric data item and since we have declared it to be a **memberCaption**, we need to convert it into a character string.]

5. In the lower-right panel under **Source**, click on the ellipsis(**...**) button under the **Source** heading:

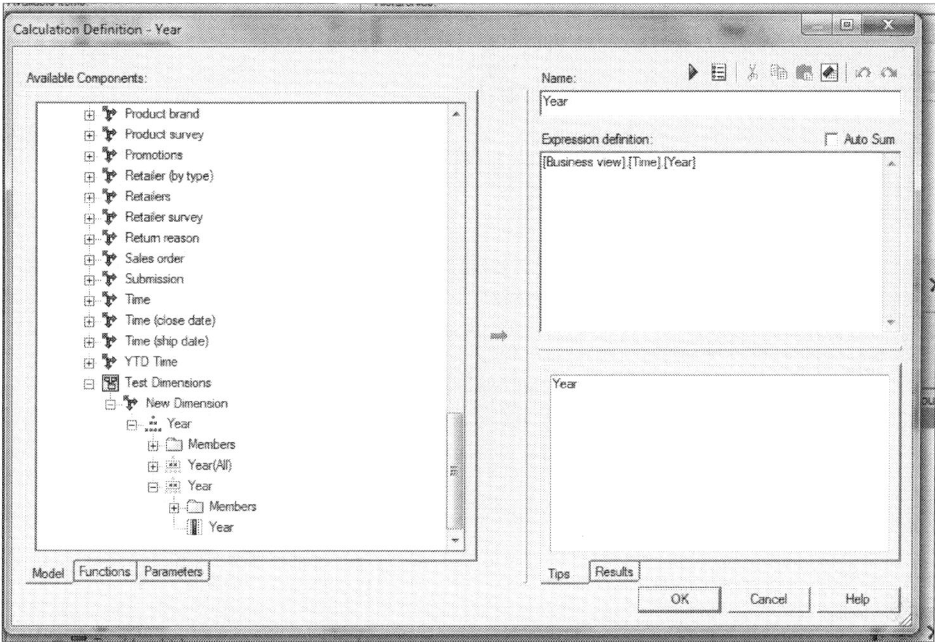

6. In the **Expression definition** box, enter the expression `CAST([Business view].[Time].[Year],CHAR(4))` and click on the **OK** button.

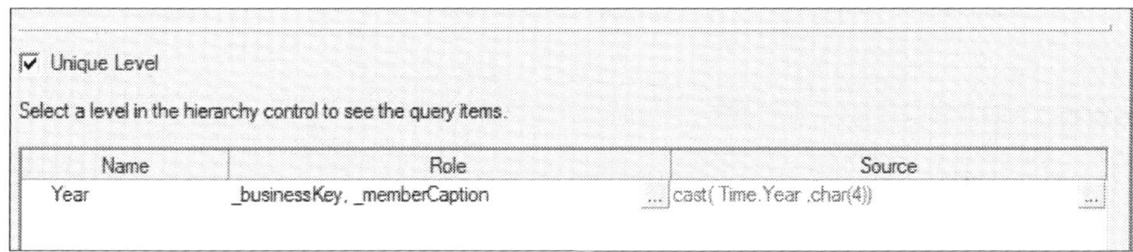

7. Ensure that the **Unique Level** checkbox is checked as shown in the preceding screenshot.
8. Right-click on the **Year** top label in the **Hierarchies** panel and rename the item to `Time`. Similarly rename `Year(all)` to `Time`.

9. Drag-and-drop the **Quarter key** label to the **Hierarchies** panel. Also drag-and-drop **Quarter, Quarter (caption)** and **Quarter (numeric)** to the lower right-panel. Make **Quarter key** into the **_businessKey** role, and **Quarter (caption)** into the **_memberCaption** role. Rename the **Quarter key** in the **Hierarchies** panel to **Quarter**, and mark the level as unique by checking the **Unique level** checkbox:

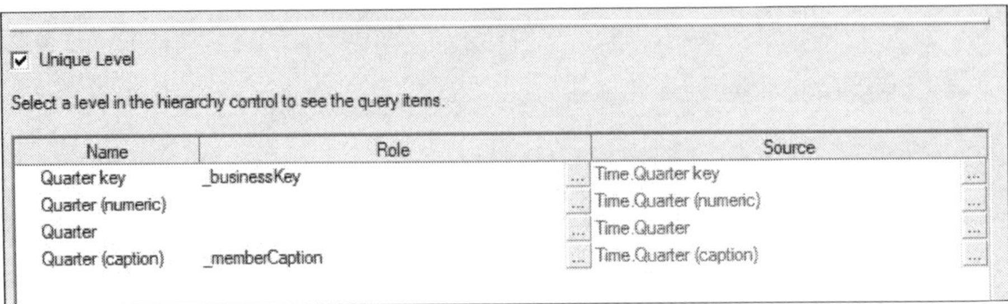

10. Perform the same procedure for **Month key**:

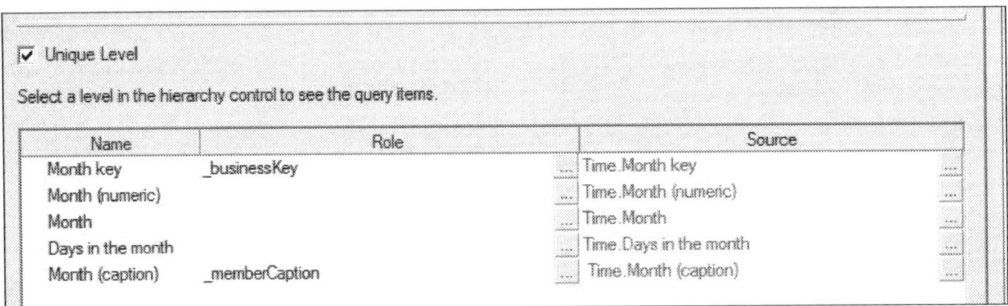

11. Select the **Member Sort** tab, check the **Data** checkbox, and select **Always (OLAP compatible)** for the sort options.
12. Select each layer in turn and select **Level Sort Properties**: **Year, Quarter key**, and **Month key**.
13. Click on **OK** and rename your new dimension to **Time** rather than the default name **New Dimension**.

Dimensions with multiple hierarchies

When you create a dimension and if you are not restricted to a single hierarchy, a dimension can have more than one hierarchy. The only restriction on using hierarchies from the same dimension is that you cannot use one hierarchy for the rows, and another hierarchy for the columns in the same crosstab. If you need to use your hierarchies in this way then each hierarchy must be in a separate dimension.

An example of multiple hierarchies for the same dimension is the time hierarchy, which can be viewed by Quarter or by Month. These hierarchies are separate but are interchangeable, and are bound to the same underlying query.

You are not limited to two hierarchies in a dimension. A dimension may contain any number of hierarchies.

The following is the **Time** dimension as a single dimension with two hierarchies, one by Month and the other by Quarter:

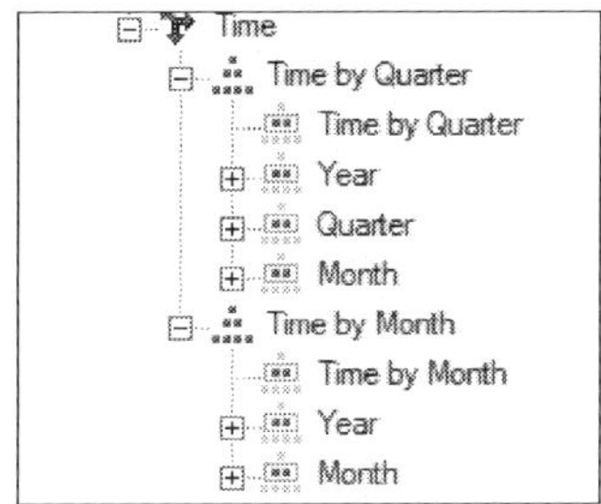

The hierarchies are defined in Framework Manager as follows:

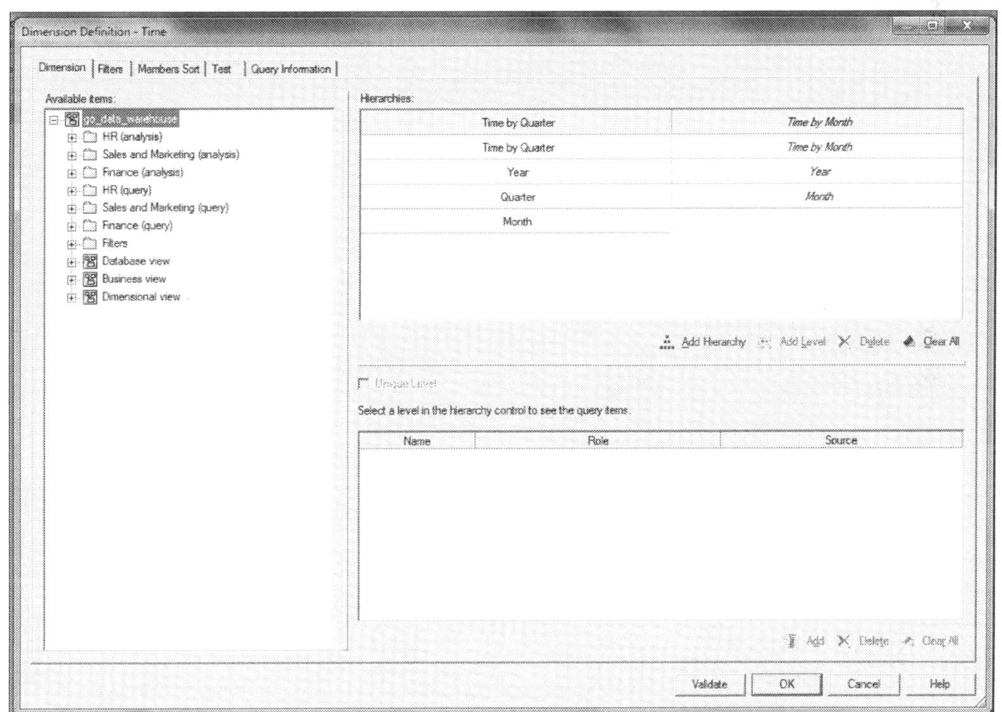

Notice that at the lowest level we need to have a common element in both the hierarchies, and in this case, Month is the common element.

Creating a multiple hierarchy dimension

To create the multiple hierarchy dimension first create a regular dimension. We will extend the regular dimension created above:

1. After creating the regular dimension, click on the **Add Hierarchy** label below the **Hierarchies** panel and it will show the following:

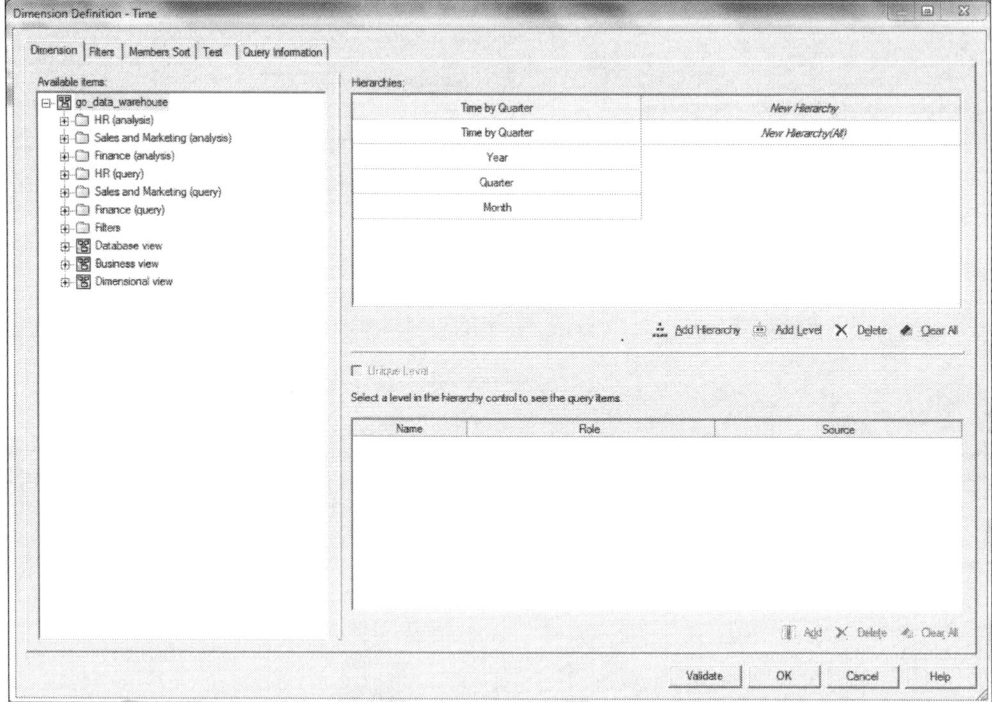

2. Drag-and-drop **Year** onto the new hierarchy, and set the **_businessKey** and **_memberCaption** attributes in the same way you did for the regular dimension.
3. Drag-and-drop **Month** below the **Year** level, the same as for the regular dimension, and drag-and-drop the **_memberCaption** attributes, the same as for the regular dimension.

4. Select the **Member Sort** tab, and define the **Year** and **Month key** as **Level Sort Properties**. When you have finished, your dimension will look like the following screenshot:

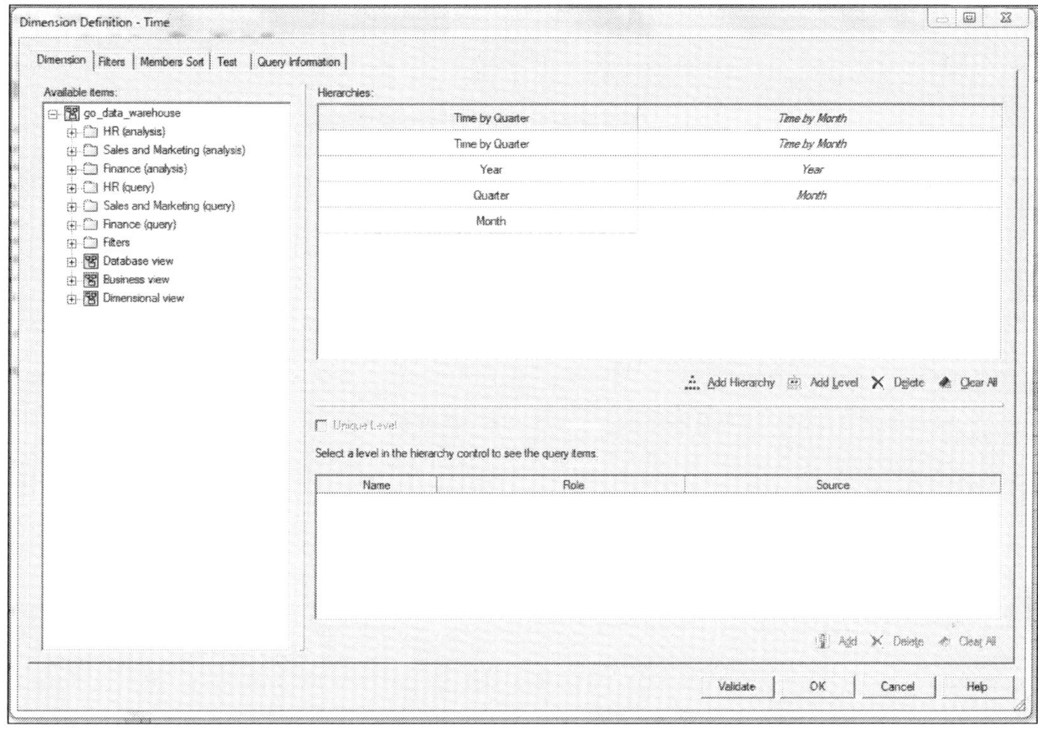

5. Click **OK** when finished and rename your new dimension.

Measure dimensions

A **measure dimension** is a collection of facts. A measure dimension is created from one or more query subjects that have a valid relationship between them.

Measure dimensions should only be composed of quantitative items and they do not contain any keys with which join them together. Therefore, to join a measure dimension to a regular dimension, it is necessary to create the joins in the underlying query subjects.

Creating a measure dimension

We will create a measure dimension using the great_outdoors_warehouse from the IBM Cognos Samples. From the model, we will use the Inventory Fact query from the Business View as a relational data source to build our measure dimension.

We will create a measure dimension as follows:

1. Right-click on your namespace, and navigate to **Create | Measure Dimension**, or alternatively click on your namespace and from the **Actions** menu, navigate to **Create | Measure Dimension**. This will show the following dimension definition dialog:

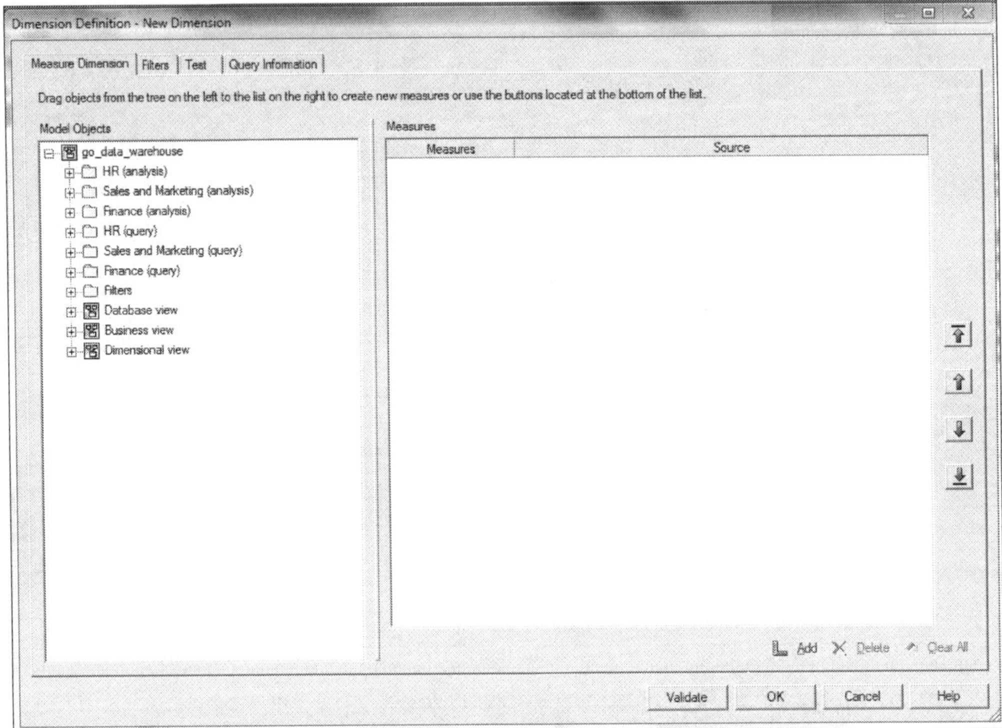

2. Navigate to **Business view** | **Inventory fact**, and drag-and-drop the following items: **Opening inventory**, **Quantity shipped**, **Additions**, **Unit cost**, and **Closing inventory** to the **Measures** pane:

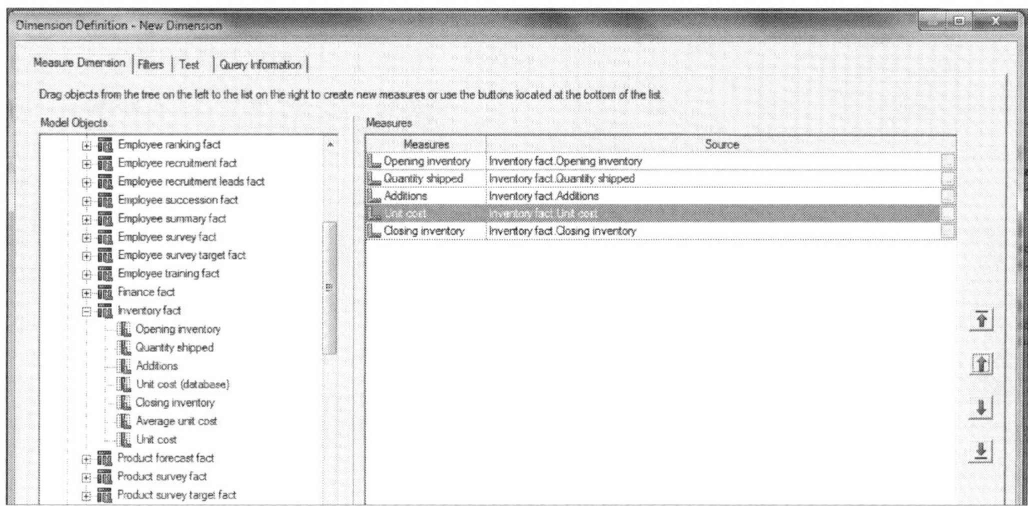

3. Click on **OK**, and give your measure dimension a name.

Creating aggregation rules for measures

For dimensionally modeled relation measures, you can define an aggregation rule called a semi-additive measure, which only relates to one specific measure and is not summed across all dimensions. These rules are in addition to any regular aggregation rules applied to the measures.

For example, inventory stock is usually recorded with a monthly opening and closing stock balance. To report an inventory for different time periods, you need to apply an aggregate that takes the value for the appropriate time within the period. For an opening stock balance the inventory stock is the last balance of the previous month, and for a closing stock balance the inventory stock is the last balance for the current month. The inventory measure has a regular aggregate of the total and an aggregate for the time dimension with a last value.

[You will need the **Properties** panel visible to be able to do this.]

To create this semi-additive measure, perform the following steps:

1. In the **Project Viewer** panel, click on the **Open Inventory** measure in your measure dimension.

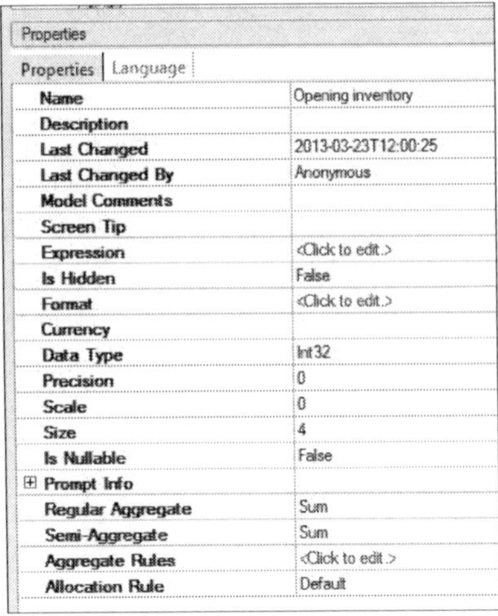

2. In the **Properties** pane, click on the **<Click to edit>** label next to **Aggregate Rules** as seen in the preceding screenshot.
3. To add a dimension for this measure, click on **Add** and select the **Time** dimension created previously:

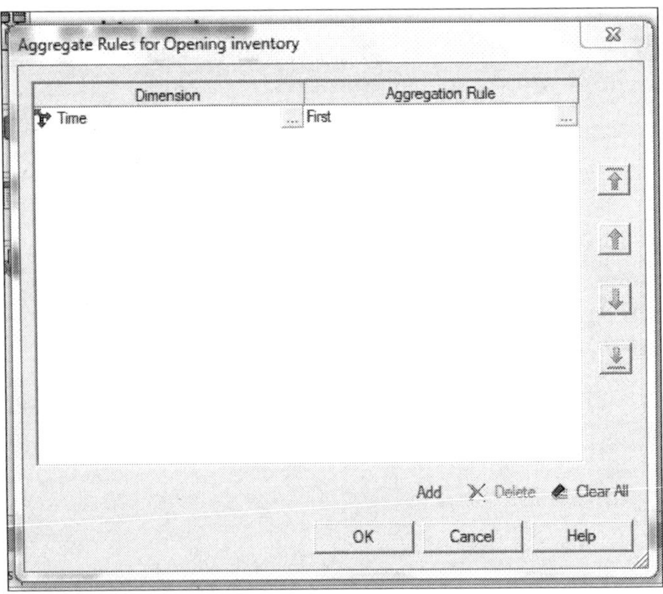

4. To specify the aggregate operation, click on the ellipsis **(...)** button in the **Aggregation Rules** box as seen in the following screenshot:

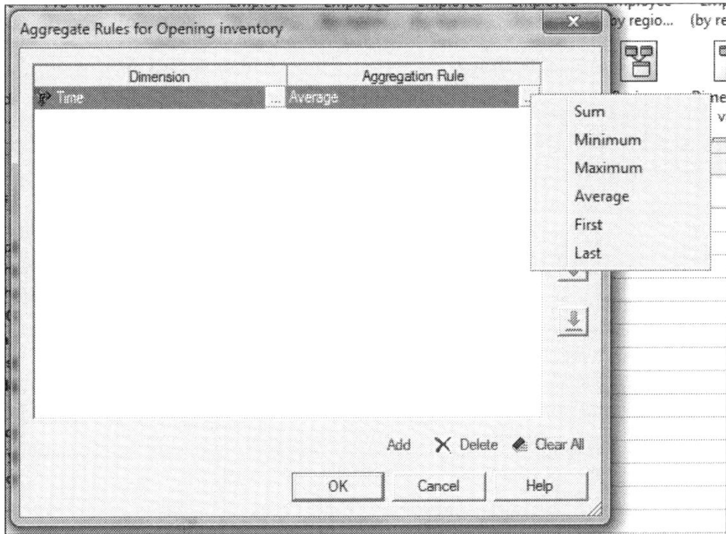

5. The following operations are supported:
   - **Sum**: This sums the values in the measure, and it is the default.
   - **Minimum**: This shows the minimum value in the measure.
   - **Maximum**: This shows the maximum value in the measure.
   - **Average**: This shows the average value in the measure.
   - **First**: This shows the first value in the measure, and it is only relevant when we have a Time dimension in the model.
   - **Last**: This shows the last value in the measure, and it is only relevant when we have a time dimension in the model.
6. In this case, select **Last** and click on **OK**.

Scope relationships

Scope relationships exist between measure dimensions and regular dimensions. These are used to define the level at which the measures are available for reporting.

Scope relationships are not the same as joins in relational queries. There are no conditions or criteria in a scope relationship that dictate how a query is to be formed. A scope relationship only specifies if a fact can be queried with a specific dimension. If there is no scope relationship between the fact and the dimension, this will result in an error.

Once you set the scope relationship for a measure dimension, the settings apply to all measures within the measure dimension. If data is to be reported at different levels for each measure in a measure dimension, then you can set the scope for each measure.

When setting the scope for a measure you are specifying the lowest level that the data can be reported on.

> If you create the measure dimensions and regular dimensions in the same namespace, Framework Manager will automatically detect and set the scope relationships.

When you create a measure dimension, Framework Manager will detect and create a scope relationship between the new measure dimension and any existing regular dimensions in the model. The scope relationships created by Framework Manager may not be the one ones you intended, and in this case you may need to modify the scope relationships.

To check the scope relationship for a measure, click on the **Show Scope** button on the toolbar.

If you change the **Project** pane to show **Diagram**, you can see if the measure and dimensions are in scope. You will see the screenshot similar to the following:

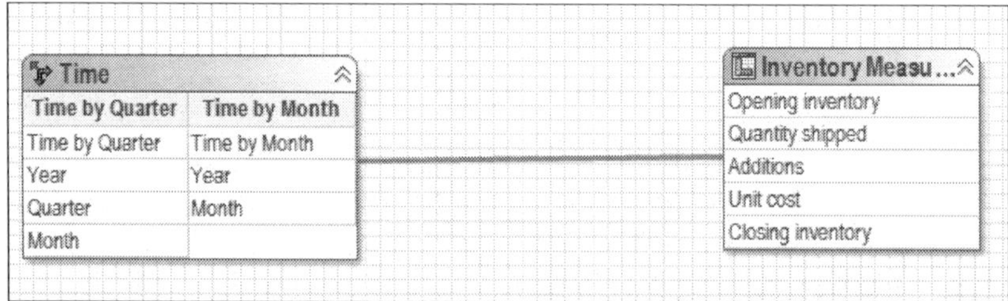

You can see from the preceding screenshot that our newly created **Inventory Measures** are "in scope" with the **Time** dimension created previously.

Creating a scope relationship

Scope relationships are usually created automatically but sometimes it is necessary to change the scope relationships or to create them manually.

To create a scope relationship, perform the following steps:

1. Change the **Project** pane to show the **Dimension Map** option:

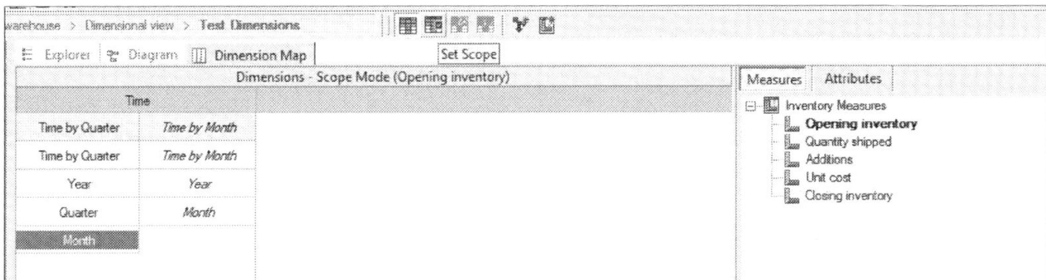

2. Select the **Measure**, for example, **Opening Inventory** and the lowest level of the dimension, where the measure is to be "in scope".
3. Click on the **Set Scope** button on the toolbar.

Summary

In this chapter, we have covered the techniques used to create a dimensional data model using a relational data source. We have covered the creation of dimensions, including dimensions with multiple hierarchies, measures, and scope relationships.

By using the techniques in this chapter, we can produce a Framework model that we can use with IBM Cognos Analysis Studio. We can also use the Framework model with Query Studio and Studio.

In the next chapter, we will look at enhancing our model by creating the business and presentation layers, which we will later publish for use by our report authors.

6

Creating the Business and Presentation Layers

This chapter will cover the creation of the business and presentation layers. The business layer is where we apply various business information rules to our model. The presentation layer is what the report author will see in Report Studio, Query Studio, and Analysis Studio.

This chapter will cover the following topics:

- Specifying attributes
- Renaming columns
- Adding prompts
- Adding filters
- Adding calculations
- Adding formatting to data items
- Using folders and namespaces for grouping information
- Using shortcuts to include the same information in different places

By the end of this chapter, users will have created the business layer and extended the usefulness of their model by adding prompts, filters, calculations, and formatting to their model. Users will also have created the presentation layer ready to be used by report authors.

Creating the business layer

The Framework Manager modeler can make the job of the report author easier by incorporating business information rules into the model. These business information rules can be as simple as renaming the columns in the imported tables to give them more intuitive names, or setting specific formatting for the imported columns. To assist the report authors, we can add standard prompts for type-in values, and standard filters, which can be reused in many different reports. We can also add calculations so that the report author does not need to add these calculations into their reports.

Renaming columns

This is perhaps the simplest task we can perform, and is often overlooked, but is perhaps the most useful thing the modeler can do. In most imported relational databases, the column names will be in all capitals, perhaps with underlines separating the various elements of the column names. These column names do not make it obvious what the data in the column is used for. The first task of the modeler is to make these column names more meaningful for the report author.

There are no specific rules for column names; the only thing to remember is that column name will be used as the default column name in reports.

To rename columns in your model, perform the following steps:

1. Select the column to rename.
2. Right-click on the column, and from the pop-up menu choose **Rename**.
3. Enter the new column name.

Hiding columns

Sometimes your model contains columns that you do not want your report authors to see, probably because they do not show anything meaningful to the report author. It is useful to hide these columns so that the report author will not see them and include them in any reports.

The columns can simply be deleted from the model, but sometimes it is better to hide the columns in case they are needed in the future.

To hide columns in your model, perform the following steps:

1. Select the column to hide.
2. In the properties panel, locate the **IsHidden** property, and change the property to **True**.

It is possible to hide multiple columns at the same time.

3. Select all the columns you want to hide and set the **IsHidden** property of the first item to **True**.
4. Using the small down arrow below the **IsHidden** property, drag the property over all the remaining selected items.

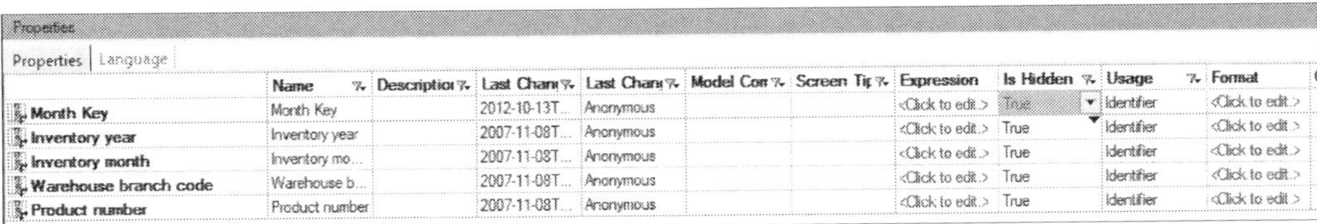

Specifying attribute types

When you import relational data into your Framework Manager model, the attribute type for each imported column is set as follows:

Data type	Attribute type
Numeric items	Fact
Date	Identifier
Character	Attribute
Blob	Unknown

This does not suit all situations since columns on database tables are often numeric data types, but they should not be considered as facts as they may be identifiers or attributes, and if they are left as facts, this may have unexpected results when they are used in reports. For example, Report Studio may total up these attribute columns to give a meaningless number. It is therefore necessary to review and set the correct attribute types of all imported data items to ensure they are set correctly.

Attribute types are specified in the properties of an item.

Expand the properties pane before working with a property's attribute types.

1. Select the data item.
2. In the properties pane, locate the **Usage** property.
3. Click on the attribute label, and from the drop-down list, select the appropriate attribute from the following:
    - **Fact**
    - **Identifier**
    - **Attribute**
    - **Unknown**

If you select multiple items, you can easily set the **Usage Property** setting for all the selected items by changing the **Usage** setting for the first item and then dragging the usage over all the remaining items by selecting the small down arrow below the changed usage property.

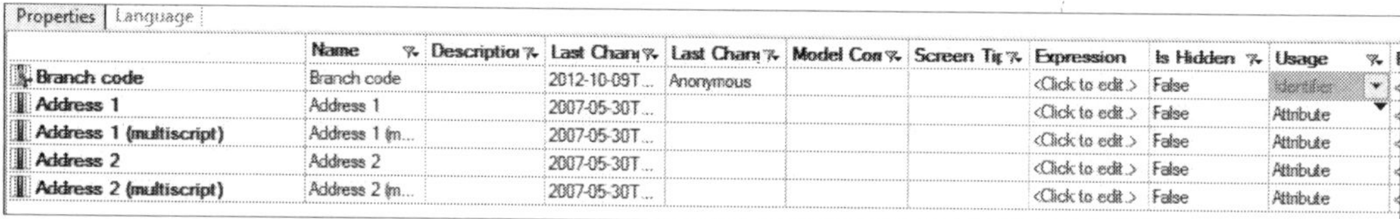

Adding filters

A filter is an expression that provides the conditions that rows must meet to be retrieved for the query subject of the report to which the filter is applied.

There are two types of filters that can be added to your Framework Manager model:

- Embedded filters
- Standalone filters

Embedded filters

Embedded filters are created within individual query subjects and they will only have an effect on the query subject within which they are embedded.

If you use embedded filters in a query subject, they should be added to the import layer.

Creating an embedded filter

To create an embedded filter, perform the following steps:

1. Double-click on the query to which the filter is to be added. This will open the **Query Subject Definition - Inventory** dialog box:

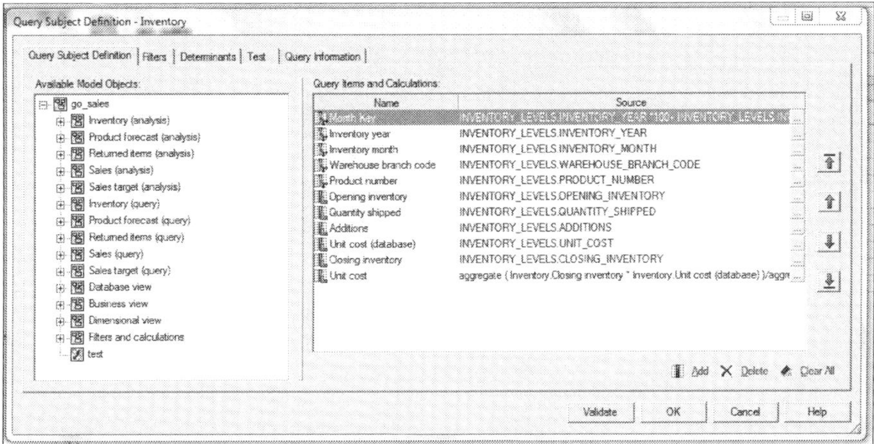

2. Select the **Filters** tab:

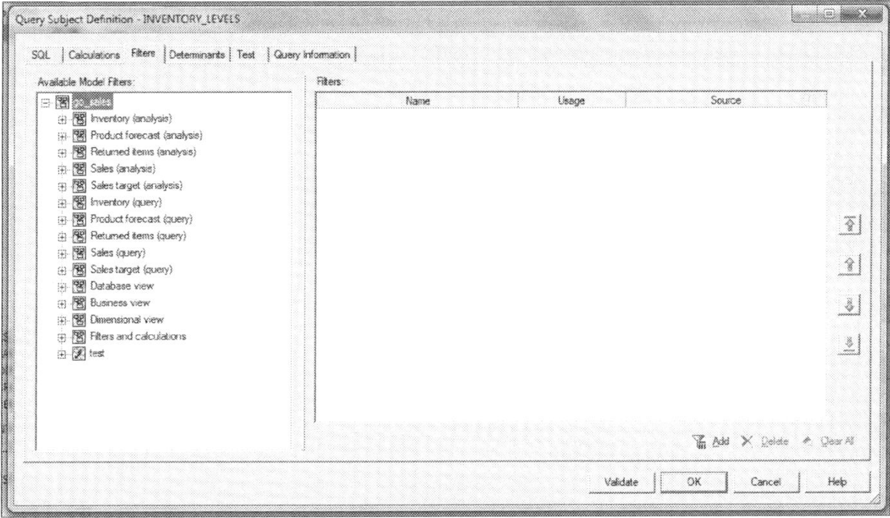

3. Click on **Add** to add your filter definition.

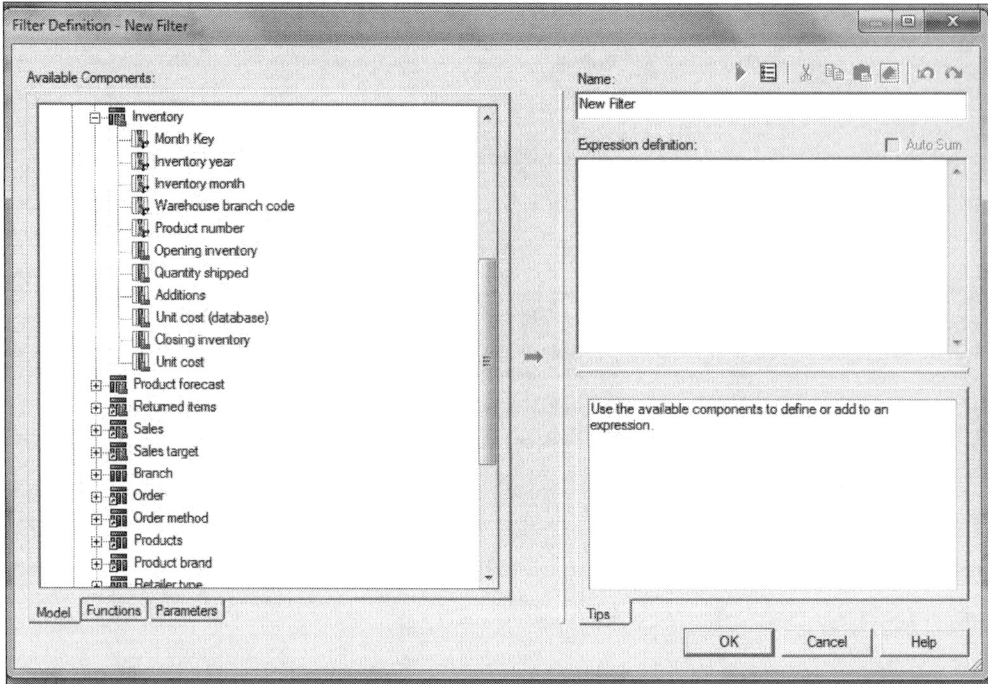

4. Give your filter a name if required—the default name will be **New Filter**.
5. From the **Available Components** box, drag-and-drop items into the **Expressions** definition box.

   If you need to use functions or parameters, click on the corresponding tab in the **Available Components** box and you can select the functions or parameters to use.

   As you drag-and-drop the items into the **Expression definition** box, the expression will be validated and error messages will appear in the **Tips** box.

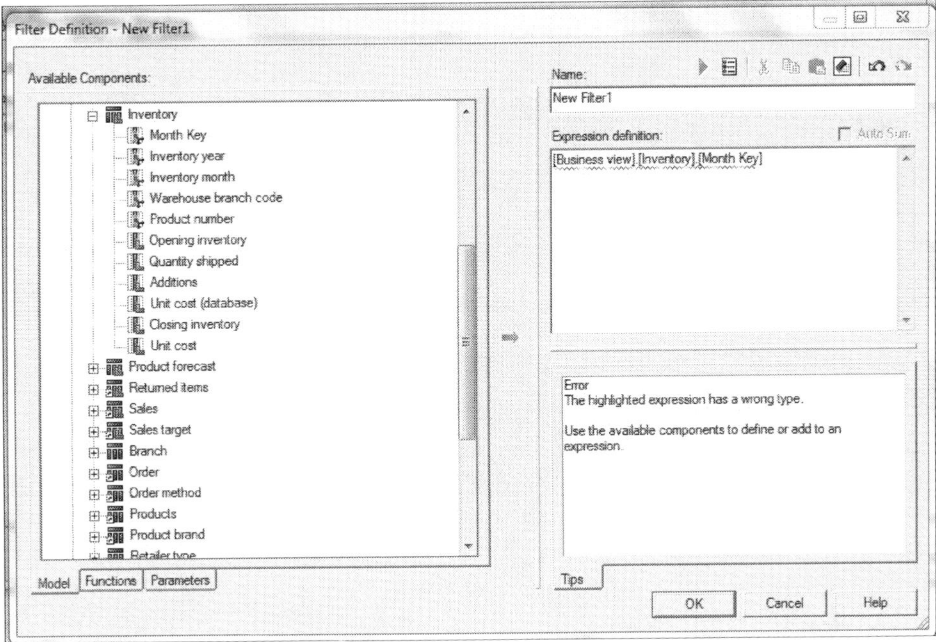

6. Once a valid filter expression has been created in the **Expression definition** box, click on the **OK** button to confirm your filter.
7. Click on the **OK** button in the query definition dialog to confirm the query.

Standalone filters

Standalone filters are filters that are available across the model. They are commonly used to make filters available to report authors, but can also be used to filter multiple query subjects within the model.

Creating a standalone filter

To create a standalone filter, perform the following steps:

1. Select the location where you want to create your filter.
2. Right-click on the location and from the pop-up menu, choose **Create** | **Filter**, or from the menu choose **Action** | **Create** | **Filter**.

3. This will show the **Filter Definition** dialog:

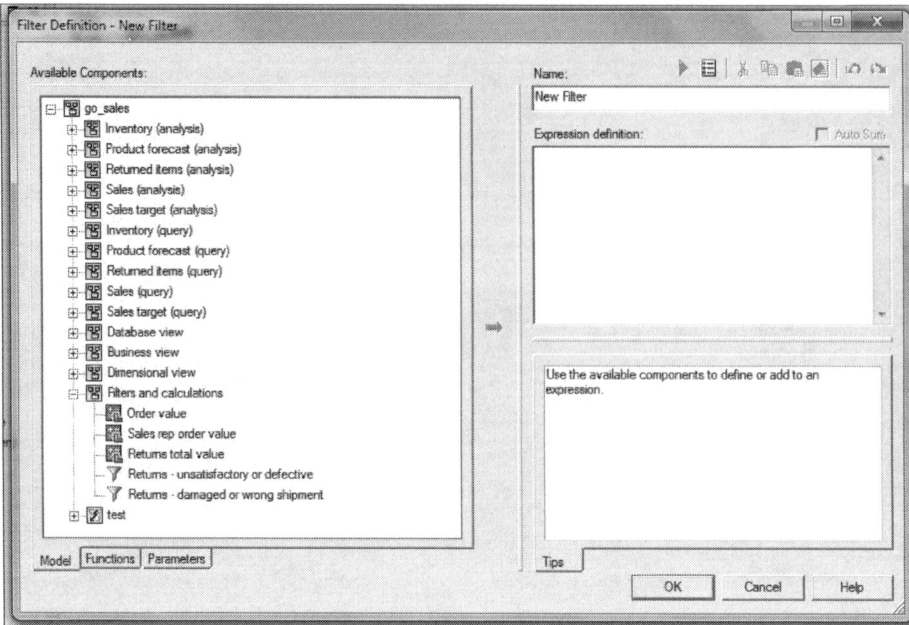

4. Give your filter a name—the default name will be **New Filter**.

> Since this is a standalone filter, which is available to report authors, the name should help identify the purpose of the filter, for example, Returns, Unsatisfactory, and Invalid Orders.

5. From the **Available Components** box, drag-and-drop items into the **Expressions definition** box.

   If you need to use functions or parameters, click on the corresponding tab in the **Available components** window and select the function or parameter to use.

As you drag-and-drop the items into the **Expression definition** box, the expression will be validated and error messages will appear in the **Tips** box.

Your filter must result in a Boolean (true or false) result; an example of a valid expression is `[GO data].[GO_TIME_DIM].[CURRENT_YEAR] = 2004`.

6. Once a valid filter expression has been created in the **Expression definition** box, click on the **OK** button to confirm your filter.

Adding calculations

You can create calculations to provide your report authors with regularly used calculated values. The calculations can use any query items, parameters, other calculations, and functions that are available within the model.

Do not use characters that are commonly used for expression operators for your calculation's name; for example, a calculation named *Rate * 10* may cause errors when used in an expression such as *[Rate * 10] < 20*.

There are two types of calculations that can be added to your model:

- Embedded calculations
- Standalone calculations

Embedded calculations

To create a calculation that is specific to a single query subject or dimension, you can embed the calculation directly in that object.

It is recommended that you apply calculations in model query subjects wherever possible, since this makes maintenance easier.

Creating embedded calculations

Embedded calculations are usually part of a query. To create an embedded calculation, perform the following steps:

1. Double-click on the query subject to which you want to add the calculation.

2. Click on the **Add** button:

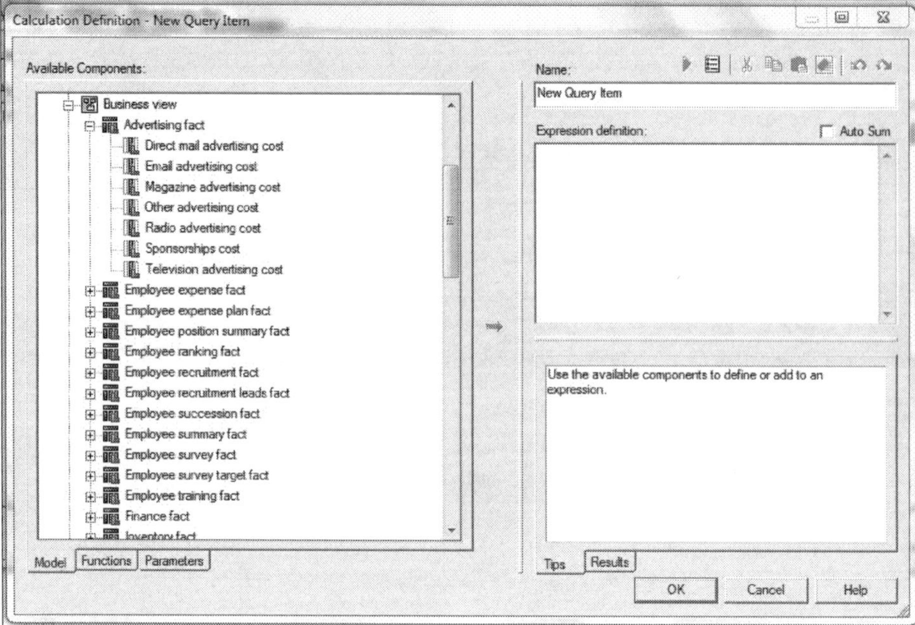

3. Give your new query item a name—the default name is **New Query Item**.
4. Drag-and-drop components from the **Available Components** box into the **Expression definition** box.

   As components are dragged, the **Tips** box will show validation errors.

   You may drag items from the **Functions** and **Parameters** tabs in the **Available components** box.

5. Once you have a valid expression, select the **Results** tab below the **Expression definition** box, and click on the small blue triangle above the **Name** box.
6. A sample of the calculation's results will be displayed in the **Results** tab below the **Expression definition** box.
7. When your expression is valid, click on **OK** to confirm.
8. Click on **OK** to confirm your changes to the query definition.

Standalone calculations

When you need to do aggregation before performing the calculation, create a standalone calculation. Change the **Regular Aggregation** property of the calculation to **Calculated**.

[Create a folder to hold all your standalone calculations so that they can be easily found by report authors.]

Creating standalone calculations

Standalone calculations are not related to any query. To create a standalone calculation, perform the following steps:

1. Select where to create the calculation.
2. Right-click on the location and choose **Create** | **Calculation**, or from the menu choose **Action** | **Create** | **Calculation**.
3. This will show the **Calculation Definition** dialog.
4. Drag-and-drop items from the **Available components** box into the **Expression definition** box.
5. When the expression definition is complete, click on OK to confirm.

Adding prompts

Prompts are generally defined in reports, but they can also be defined in the model. This is useful for items that are not shown on the report, but are used only for filtering data.

Prompts are a special type of filters. You add your prompts in the same way as you add filters to your model.

[Since the prompts are being made available to your report authors, you should create them as standalone filters, and put them with your other standalone filters.]

1. Select where you are going to create your prompt.
2. Right-click on the location and choose **Create** | **Filter**, or form the menu choose **Action** | **Create** | **Filter**.

3. Create your prompt filter by dragging items from the **Available components** box.
4. When you create a prompt, your expression will look slightly different to the expressions you use in normal filters, a prompt filter example is `[GO data].[GO_TIME_DIM].[CURRENT_YEAR] = ?Year?.`

   When this prompt filter is used, the report user will be prompted for `Year`.
5. When your prompt filter is complete, click on **OK** to confirm.

Creating prompts with Macros

In *Chapter 3, Importing Data Sources*, in the section *Importing Stored Procedures*, we added prompts to a stored procedure using some of the available macros within Framework Manager. We can use these same macros to create other prompts in our Framework Manager model. To create prompts using Prompt macros, perform the following steps:

1. Select where you are going to create your prompt.
2. Right-click on the location and choose **Create** | **Filter**, or from the menu choose **Action** | **Create** | **Filter**.
3. Create your filter by dragging items from the **Available Components** box.
4. Select the **Parameters** tab in the **Available Components** box.

The prompt macros are **Prompt** and **PromptMany**. When you select the macro to drag it to the **Expression definition** box, the tip box will display details about the format of the parameter.

5. Drag the **Prompt** macro from the **Available Components** box.

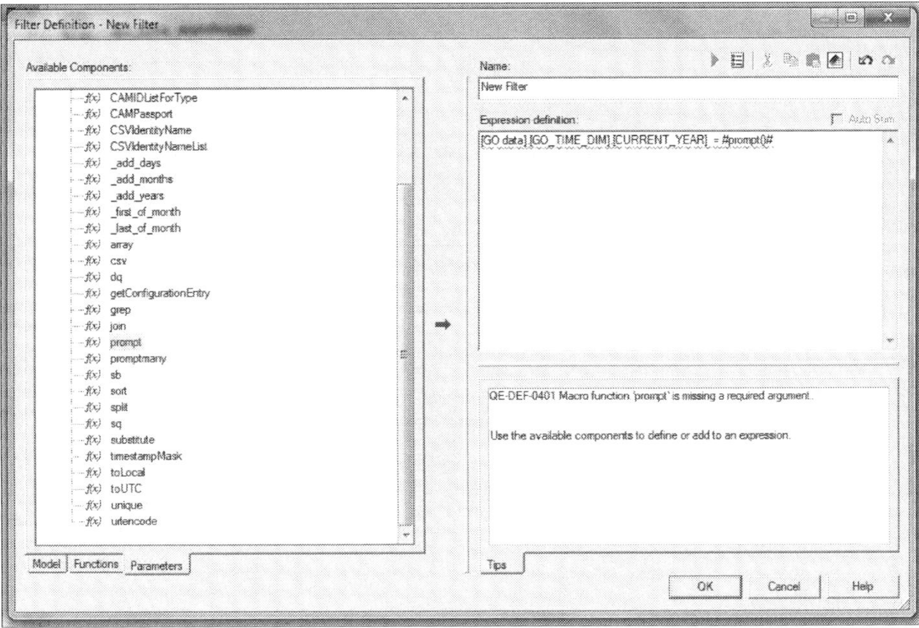

6. We need to add some additional items to our macro, and the end result should be `[GO data].[GO_TIME_DIM].[CURRENT_YEAR] = #prompt('Year', 'Integer' )#`.

> We can make the prompt required or optional by using some of the additional parameters for the macro function.
>
> The complete definition for the prompt macro is as follows:
>
> 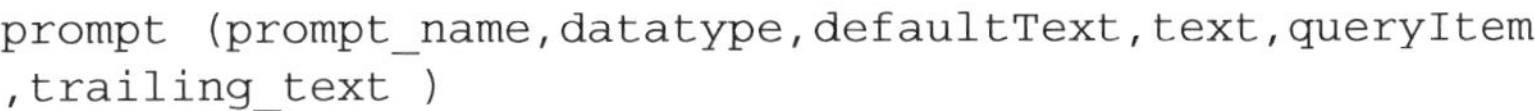
>
> ```
> prompt (prompt_name,datatype,defaultText,text,queryItem
> ,trailing_text )
> ```
>
> `prompt_name` is required. The `datatype` defaults to `string` when it is not specified. The prompt is optional when `defaultText` is specified. `text`, when specified, will precede the value. `queryItem` can be specified to take advantage of the prompt information properties of `queryItem`. `trailing_text`, when specified, will be appended to the value. When the definition is complete, click on **OK** to confirm.

Adding formatting

It is possible to add specific formatting properties to any column that has been imported into Framework Manager. This will save the report author from having to set the formatting in his/her reports.

Data formatting properties

The following is a list of properties available in the data formatting dialog:

- **Text**
- **Number**
- **Currency**
- **Percentage**
- **Date**
- **Time**
- **Date/Time**
- **Time Interval**
- **Custom**

When choosing one of these format types, a specific set of properties is available.

Using formatting patterns

Sometimes, the available formatting does not provide the formatting required for a particular situation, so each of the format types allows you to specify a formatting pattern to use.

For example, you can format dates to use full text including the era, or you can format them to only use numbers and show the last two digits of years to save space.

Using symbols and patterns can provide similar results as basic data formatting tasks. For example, you can set how many digits appear after the decimal point. You can achieve these types of results with a pattern, or you can set the **No. of Decimal Places** property. The formatting patterns allow greater flexibility for more complex formatting requirements.

When you define a formatting pattern, the number of symbols used will affect how the data is presented. There are different rules for text, numbers, and values that can be text or numbers, such as dates.

You can specify whether text is produced in full or in an abbreviated form. The following table shows the effect of the number of formatting symbols on how data is formatted:

Number of symbols	**Meaning**	**Example**
4 or more	Full text form	EEEE produces Monday
Less than 4	Abbreviated form	EEE produces Mon

The number of symbols used in the pattern sets the minimum number of digits that are shown in a report. Number that has fewer digits than specified will be zero padded; for example, if you specify a format `mm` for minutes and the database value is `6`, the report will show `06`.

For values that can be text or numbers, such as months, you can use the formatting pattern to specify whether numbers or text are printed, and whether the month names are abbreviated or not. This is shown in the following table:

Number of symbols	**Meaning**	**Example**
3 or more	Text	MMMM produces February
		MMM produces Feb
Less than 3	Numbers	MM produces 02
		M produces 2

When using pattern formatting with date and time symbols, the following patterns are available for individual date components:

Meaning	**Symbol**	**Presentation**	**Example**
Era	G	Text	AD
Year	y	Number	1996
Year (of Week of Year)	Y	Number	1996
Month in year	M	Text and number	July and 07
Week in year	w	Number	27
Week in month	W	Number	2
Day in year	D	Number	189
Day in month	d	Number 10	
Day of week in month	F	Number	2 (2nd Wed in July)
Day of Week (1=first day)	e	Number	2
Day in week	E	Text	Tuesday

Meaning	Symbol	Presentation	Example
a.m. or p.m. marker	a	Text	pm
Hour in day (1 to 24)	k	Number	24
Hour in a.m. or p.m. (0 to 11)	K	Number	0
Hour in a.m. or p.m.(1 to 12)	h	Number	12
Hour in day (0 to 23)	H	Number	0
Minute in hour	m	Number	30
Second in minute	s	Number	55
Millisecond	S	Number	978
Time zone	z	Text	Pacific Standard Time
Escape used in text	'	n/a	n/a
Single quote	''	n/a	'

When using pattern formatting for decimal numbers, the following formatting patterns can be used:

Symbol	Meaning
0	A digit that is shown even if the value is zero.
#	A digit that is suppressed if the value is zero.
.	A placeholder for decimal separator.
,	A placeholder for thousands grouping separator.
E	Separates mantissa and exponent for exponential formats.
;	Separates formats for positive numbers and formats for negative numbers.
-	The default negative prefix.
%	Multiplied by 100, as percentage.
‰	Multiplied by 1000, as per mille.
¤	The currency symbol. If this symbol is present in a pattern, the monetary decimal separator is used instead of the decimal separator.
¤¤	The international currency sign. It will be replaced by an international currency symbol. If it is present in a pattern, the monetary decimal separator is used instead of the decimal separator.
X	Other characters that can be used in the prefix or suffix.
'	Used to quote special characters in a prefix or suffix.
/u221E	Infinity symbol.

Adding formatting

Before setting formats, you may find it useful to expand the **Properties** pane to see more details, or show multiple items.

1. Select the column you want to format.

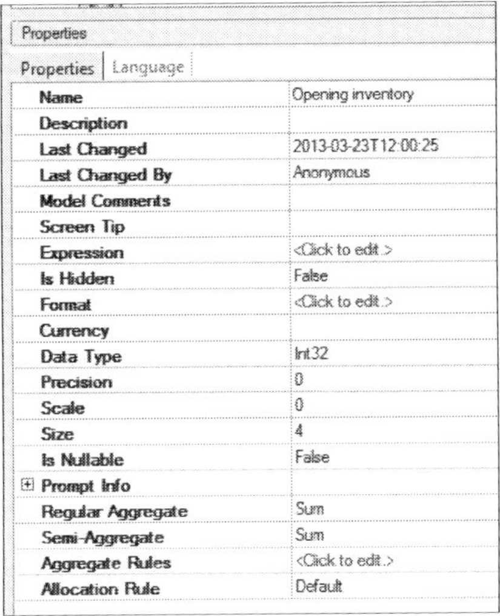

2. In the properties pane, click on the **Format** property and then click on the text labelled `<click to edit>`.
3. This will bring up the **Data Format** dialog box:

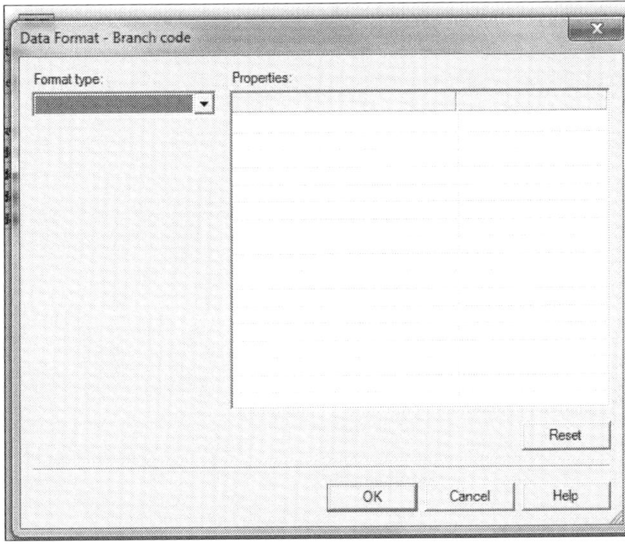

4. In the **Format type** box, select the predefined format type.

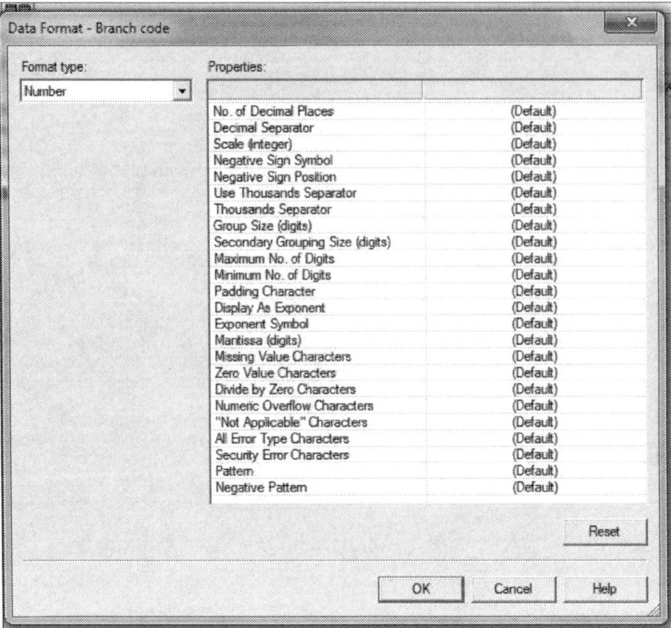

5. Change the formatting properties as required.

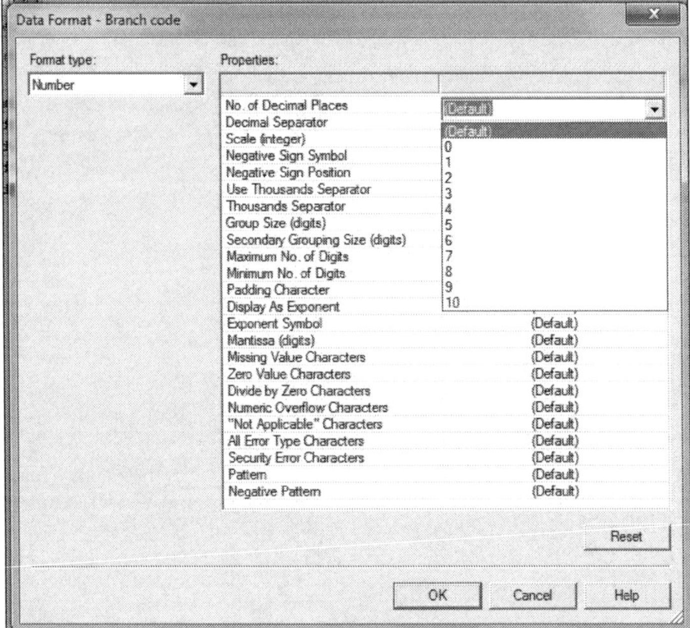

Formatting patterns may be set by selecting the **Pattern** property and entering the appropriate pattern.

6. When all formatting properties are set, click on the **OK** button to confirm the formatting choices.

[You can set the formatting of multiple items by selecting them all, changing the format for the first item in the list, and then dragging the format over all the remaining items by selecting the small down arrow below the changed format property.]

Creating the presentation layer

Once we have completed all the modeling steps, we are ready to create our presentation layer.

The presentation layer is the layer of our framework model that is available to report authors.

[Create a new namespace called Presentation Layer.]

Grouping data items

The first thing we must consider while creating our presentation layer is how to create groupings of related items. For example, order lines, order headers, customers, and order items could be a group of items that logically go together; invoice lines, invoice headers, customers, and invoiced items could be another logical group. Genrally, we would group together items that make sense from a business viewpoint.

Using folders and namespaces

In earlier chapters, we have looked at how to create namespaces and folders. When you want to group like data together, the use of namespaces and folders is essential.

Use folders to create logical groups; unless when you are using DMR, you will need to use namespaces to group the items to ensure they are in scope.

Using shortcuts

We could duplicate all the items from our business layer into our presentation layer by creating Model Query items from all the objects in our business layer. But we do not need to do this.

What we do instead is create shortcuts between the objects in our presentation layer and the objects in our business layer, and place them into our presentation layer where required. This solves the issue of data items that logically can appear in more than one grouping, such as our customers and items in the preceding example.

When we create shortcuts, we can even give our shortcuts different names so that our customer shortcut in order could be called order customers, and our customer in invoices could be called invoice customers.

Creating shortcuts

To create a shortcut from one object to another, perform the following steps:

1. Select the item to make a shortcut from.
2. Right-click on the item and select **Create | Shortcut**, or from the menu choose **Action | Create | Shortcut**.
3. Rename the shortcut to the desired name—the default name will be **Shortcut to <Object>**, for example, **Shortcut to Customers**.
4. Drag-and-drop your shortcut to the desired location.

Summary

In this chapter, we have looked at creating the business and presentation layers and making it easy for report authors by adding business information rules.

We added filters, calculations, and prompts, and set the default formatting to make our model easy to use for report authors.

Finally, we created our presentation layer by using shortcuts to existing objects rather than duplicating all the objects in our model.

We are now ready to publish our model for our report authors to use.

In the next chapter, we will look at how to create packages to publish our model for report authors to use to create their reports.

7
Creating and Publishing Packages

Once all the layers of the model have been created, we have to present the model to the report authors for them to use. This chapter covers the creation of the package, or packages, including setting up security.

The following topics are covered in this chapter:

- Creating packages
- Publishing packages
- Creating externalized query subjects
- Using package versions
- Applying security settings to packages

By the end of this chapter you will be able to create and publish a package to allow report authors to use the data model to design their reports in IBM Cognos Studios.

After creating our Framework Manager model we must now make our model available to report authors. To do this we need to create a package; the items within the package are what the report author uses to create their reports.

Once we have created the package we need to publish the package to the IBM Cognos Business Intelligence Server. During the publishing process there are various options available, including the ability to create external queries, to create versions, to add security, and to specify whether the package should use Dynamic Query Mode.

To illustrate some of the features of creating and publishing packages we will use the following model. In this model the Import Layer is called Foundation Layer, and the Modeling Layer is called Business Layer.

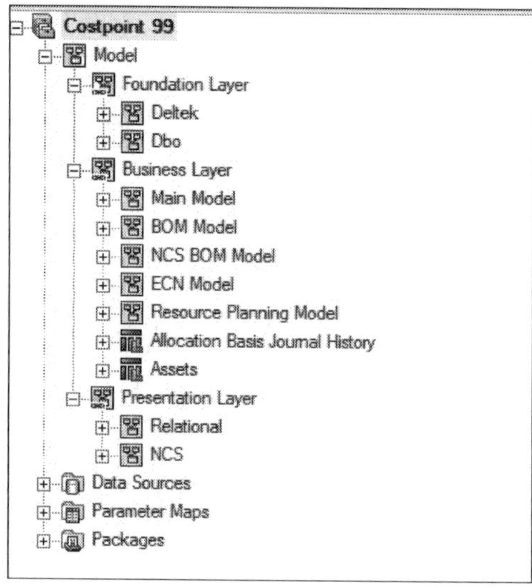

Creating a package

The first step in making our model available to report authors is the creation of a new package. A package can be created as follows:

1. In the **Package Viewer** pane of our model, select **Packages**.
2. Right-click and select **Create | Package**, or from the menu choose **Actions | Create | Package**
3. This will launch the **Create Package** wizard.

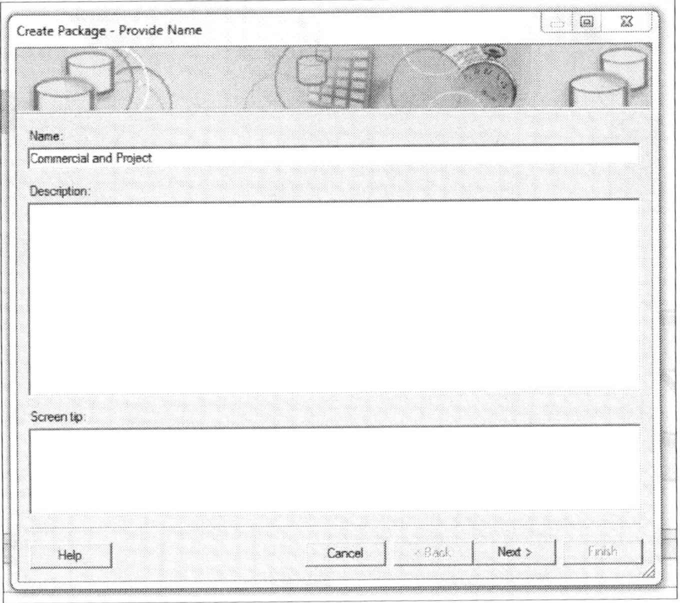

4. The first thing we must do is provide a name for the package and optionally a description and screen tip, and then click on **Next**.
5. We must now define the objects to be included in our package.

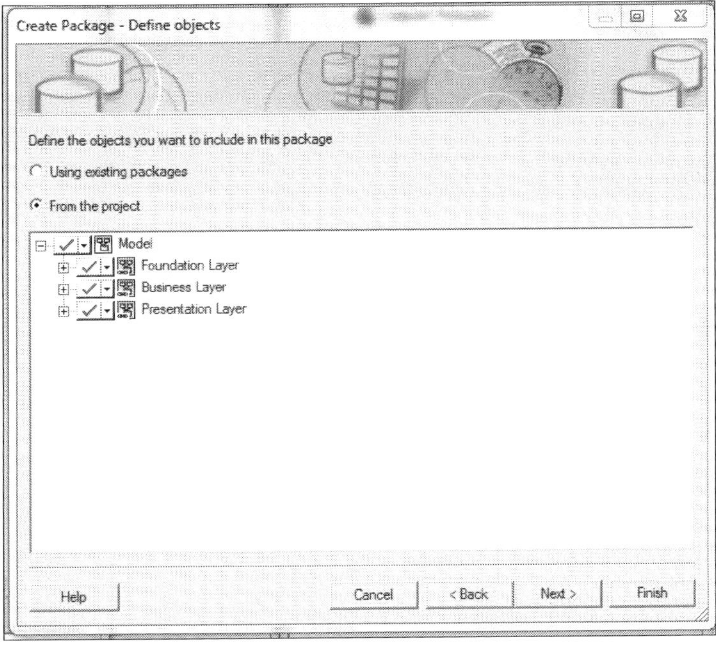

6. The current project is the default for choosing what to include in the package.
7. We do not want to include all objects in this package so click on the down arrow next to the **Foundation Layer** name; we now have the following choices:
    - **Select Component and Children** (this is the default option)
    - **Hide Component and Children**
    - **Unselect Component and Children**

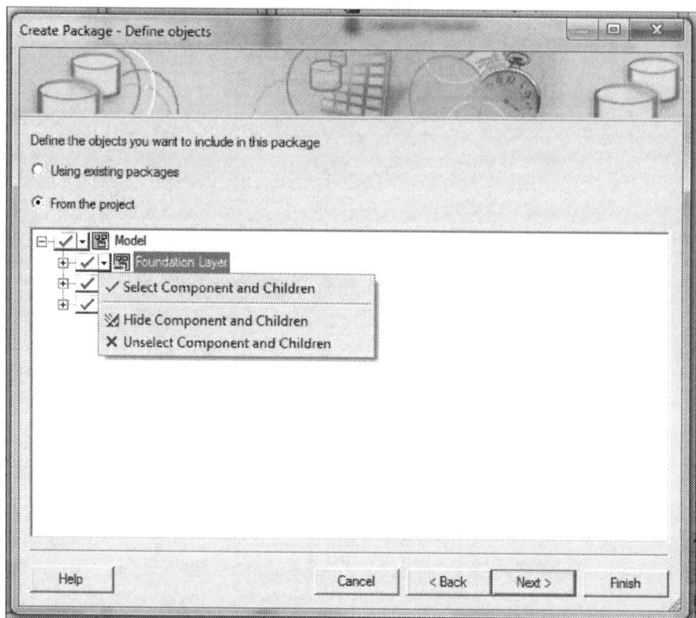

8. Use the **Hide Component and Children** option for the Import (**Foundation**) Layer, and repeat this choice for the Modeling (**Business**) Layer.

If you use the **Unselect Components and Children** option this will cause the model to generate information messages about components that need to be included in the package, because they are referenced by the components being published.

9. We do not want all the folders in the Presentation Layer to be in our package, so expand the Presentation Layer by selecting the **+** sign next to the layer name.

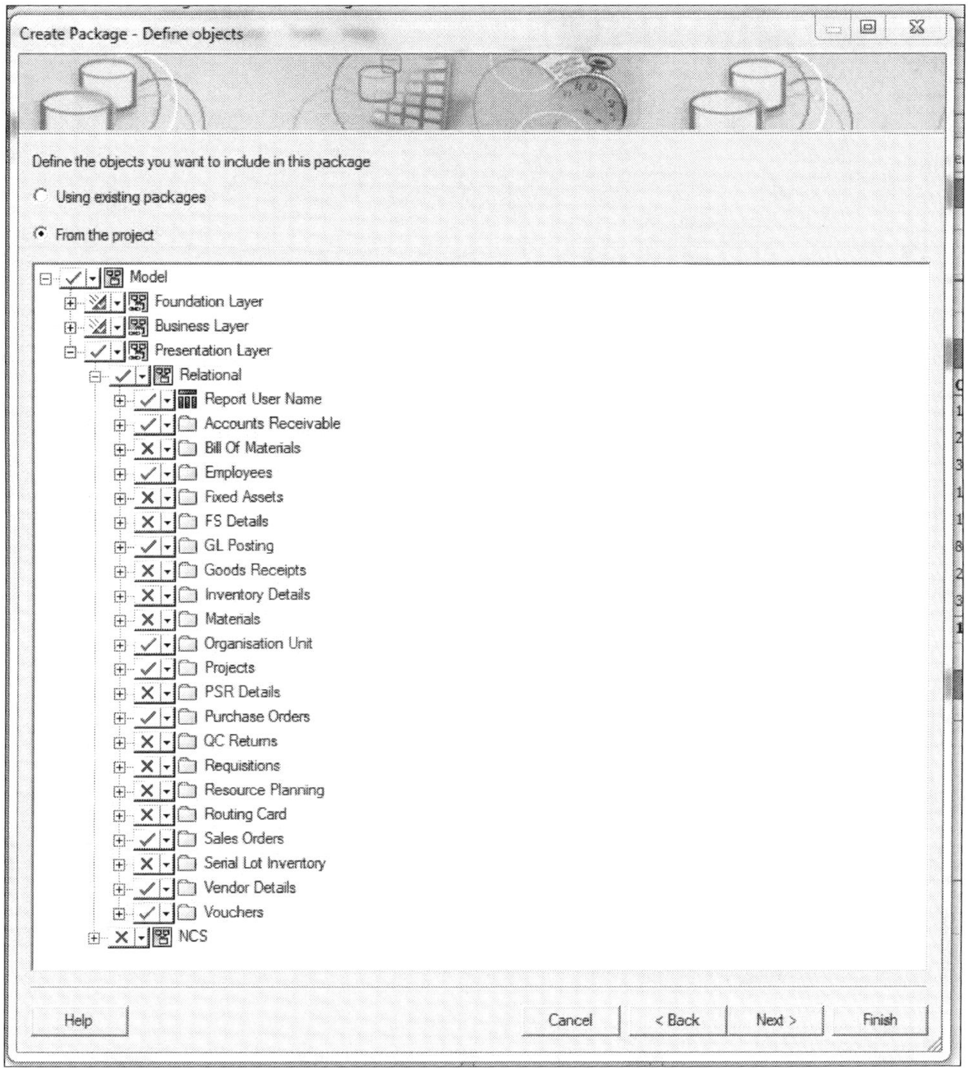

10. Exclude the folders we do not want in the final package by selecting the **Unselect Components and Children** option, and include folders by selecting the **Select Components and Children** option. Items inside the folders can be included and excluded in the same way.
11. When all objects to be included in the package have been selected, click on **Next** to continue.

12. We can now select the vendor's database functions to be included in the package.

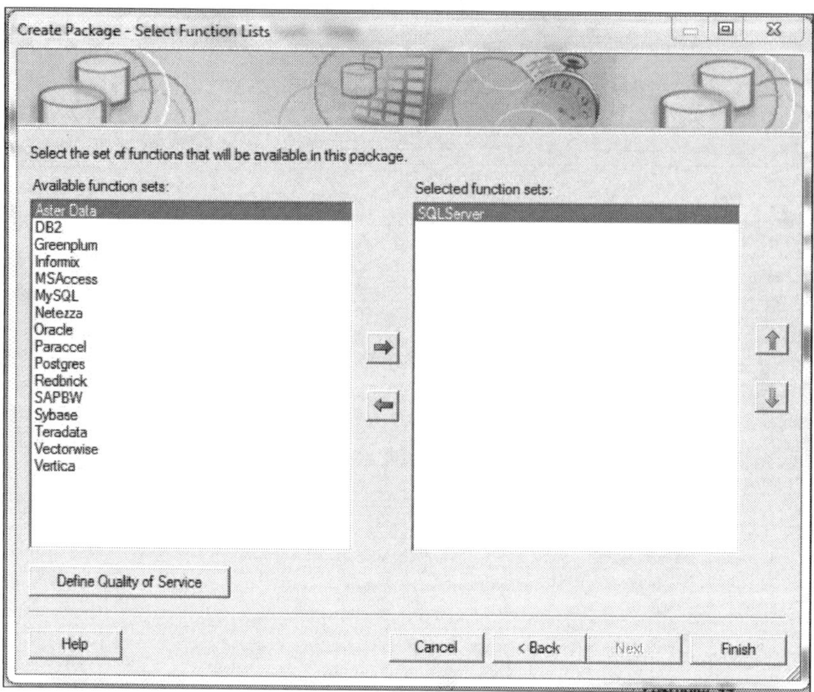

13. The function lists are selected from the **Available function sets** list on the left and transferred to the **Selected function sets** list on the right by selecting the function set and clicking on the right-pointing arrow. Unwanted function sets can be removed from the **Selected function sets** list by selecting them and pressing the left-pointing arrow.

You should only select the function lists for the database vendor you are using, for example SQL Server, Oracle, or Sybase. If your database is not in the list of available function sets then do not include any vendor functions.

If you include vendor functions that are not supported by your database then your report authors may use these functions, which could result in errors with their reports.

14. Click on **Finish** to complete your package definition.
15. When prompted to publish the newly created package, select **No**.

Making changes to a package

We can also make changes to our package as follows:

1. Right-click on the package and choose **Edit Package** from the pop-up menu; this will show the following dialog:

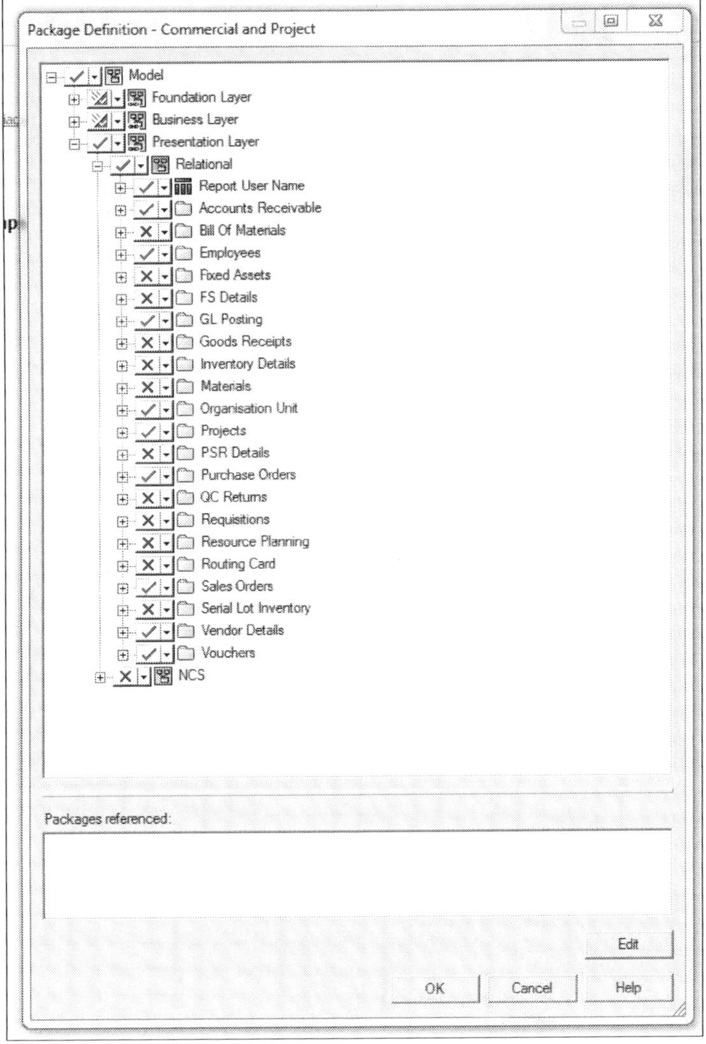

2. Click on the drop-down arrow next to the folders and choose whether to include or exclude the item, in the same way as when creating your package.
3. After making all the changes required, click on **OK** to save them.

Publishing a package

Once we have created our new package we need to publish it to the IBM Cognos Server. To publish our package perform the following steps:

1. Right-click on the package name and choose **Publish Package**.
2. This will launch the **Publish Wizard** window.

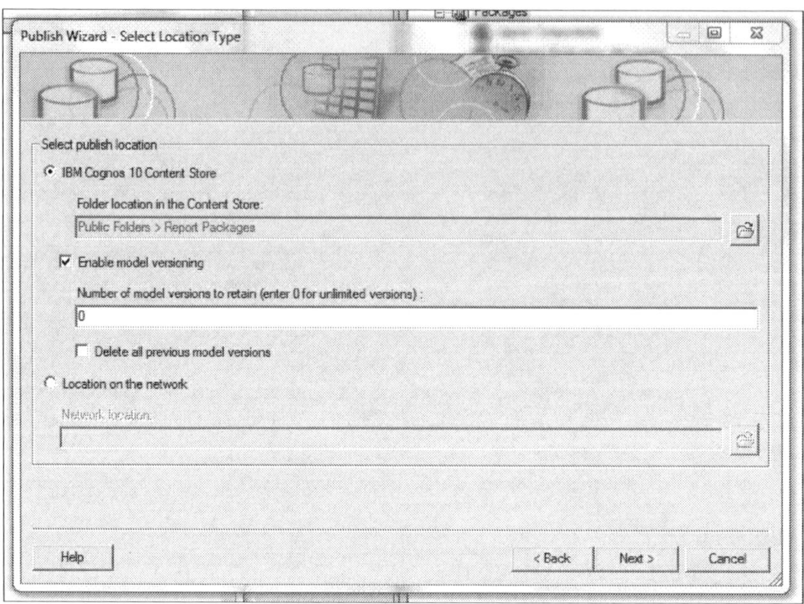

[Initially, the publish location will be set to **Public Folders**, but you can change this location and put all your packages into any folder on the IBM Cognos Server. In this case, the packages are all published into **Public Folders > Packages**. You can change the folder location by clicking on the folder icon to the right of the box labeled **Folder location in the Content Store** and selecting a new location.]

3. Select whether you want to include versioning by selecting the **Enable model versioning** checkbox, and setting the number of versions to retain.

[The **Location on the network** option is only relevant if creating externalized query subjects.]

4. Click on **Next** to continue.

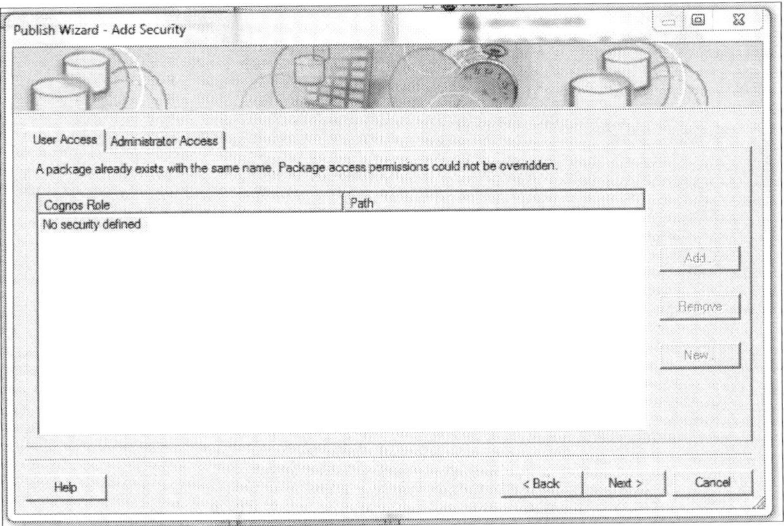

5. Initially you will be asked to set package security; if you have already published your package without any security you can click on **Next** to continue.

You can set the security on the package at a later time from the Cognos Connection screen.

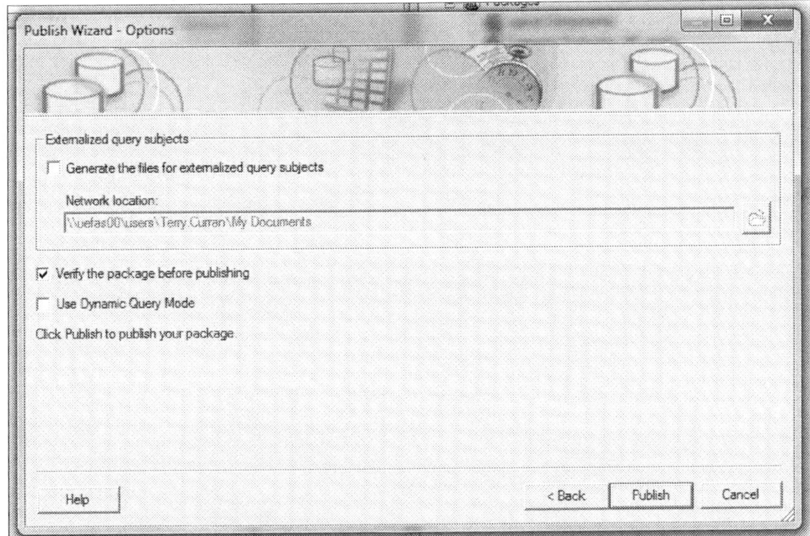

Leave the **Verify package before publishing** option checked.

6. If you are generating externalized queries select the **Generate the files for externalized query subjects** option. If you want to use the Dynamic Query mode select the **Use Dynamic Query Mode** option. These options are explained in more detail later in the chapter.

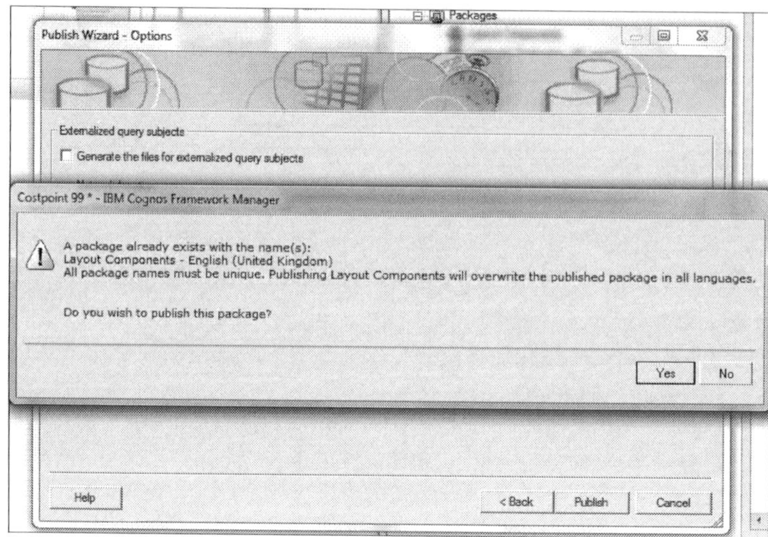

7. If you have previously published your package you will be asked to confirm overwriting the previous versions; click on the **Yes** button to confirm that you want to publish the package.

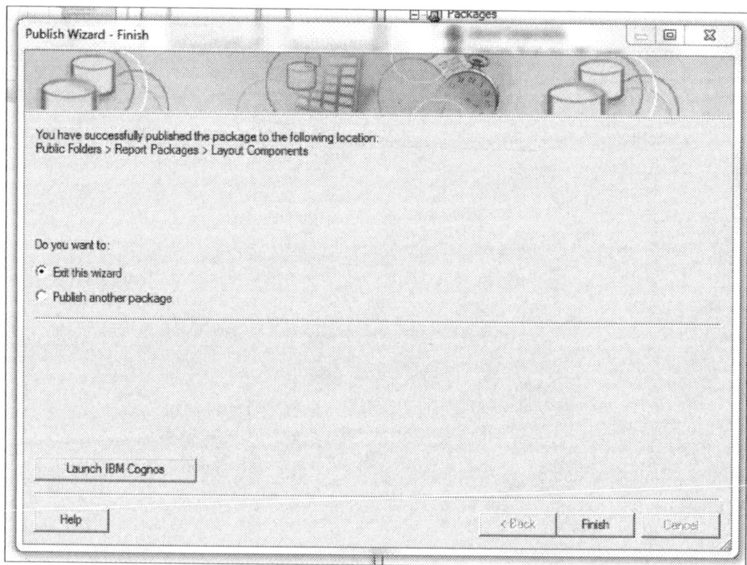

8. After your package is published, click on **Finish**. If there are information messages, warnings messages, or error messages you will have an option to review these messages after you click on **Finish**.

Information or warning messages can generally be ignored. If you have error messages then you will need to fix these before your package is published.

Using package versioning

When you publish a package to the IBM Cognos Server you have the option to create versions of the package. If you choose to create versions of your package this can be a useful feature, since you can modify your package without affecting any existing reports that use the package definition.

Any new modified report will always use the latest version of the package. After a package has been republished when a report author opens an existing report, they will be informed that the package has been modified and asked to verify the report against the latest package definition. After verifying the report the report must be saved to complete the update process for the report.

If you are working in a development environment where the Framework Model and packages are changed frequently, it is better to turn versioning off, so any new or existing reports will always use the latest package definition. In a production environment, you will probably want to turn versioning on so that any existing reports are not affected by changes to the package, but new or amended reports use the latest package.

Using externalized query subjects

During the process of publishing your package you have the option to externalize query subjects and dimensions. This allows you to create formats that can be used by IBM Cognos Transformer and other applications.

Creating externalized queries

To create externalized query subjects you have to specify how each object will be externalized.

1. Select the object to be externalized.

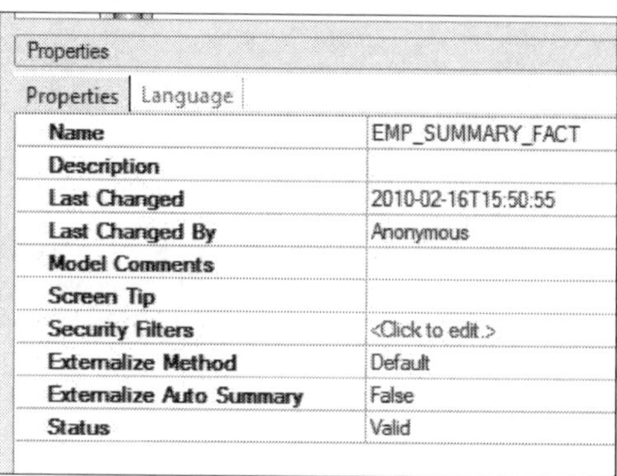

2. In the **Properties** panel for the object, click on the **Default** label next to the **Externalize Method** label.
3. Choose one of the available externalize methods. These methods are mainly for use with IBM Cognos Transformer; they may also be used for other applications. The following externalize methods are available:
    - **Default**: Use this method for objects which you do not want to externalize (this is the default method).
    - **CSV**: This method creates a comma-separated file, which contains the results of the query execution. The first row contains the column names, and each further row contains one record from the result set of the query.
    - **Tab**: This is similar to the CSV method, except each column is separated by a tab.
    - **IQD**: This method creates an IQD file for the query. The IQD definition is created specifically for use by IBM Cognos Transformer. The IQD file contains the native SQL for the query in a a format that can be imported directly into IBM Cognos Transformer.

[ The IQD method is deprecated within IBM Cognos Transformer and will be removed in future versions, so this method should no longer be used.]

Using the Dynamic Query Mode

The Dynamic Query Mode is a new feature within IBM Cognos for query optimization and enhanced query behavior. The Dynamic Query Mode is recommended for new applications of IBM Cognos Business Intelligence. You can enable the Dynamic Query Mode when creating a new Framework Manager project.

If you did not enable Dynamic Query Mode when creating the project, then it may be turned on when the package is published. If you are publishing a package from an established model that may have been created for a previous version of IBM Cognos Business Intelligence, then the package may also be published with the Dynamic Query Mode enabled.

To enable Dynamic Query Mode in your package select the **Use Dynamic Query Mode** checkbox when publishing your package.

When you publish your package with Dynamic Query Mode enabled, you will be asked to confirm that you wish to publish your package with Dynamic Query Mode before publishing the package.

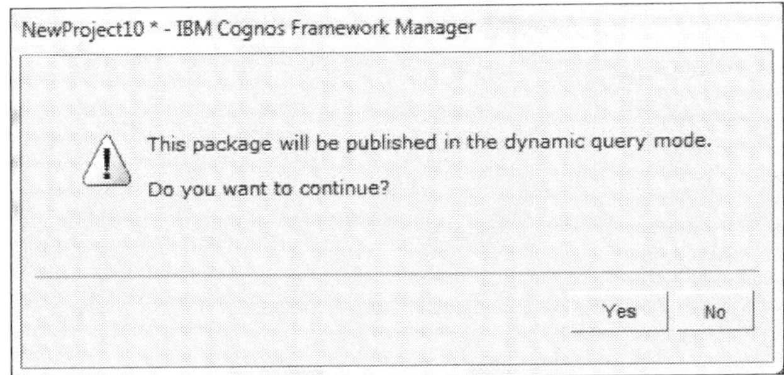

When prompted, click on the **Yes** button to publish your package with the Dynamic Query Mode.

Using package security

You can apply security to a package and identify who has access to that package. During the initial publishing process you can specify the package security settings to add to the package.

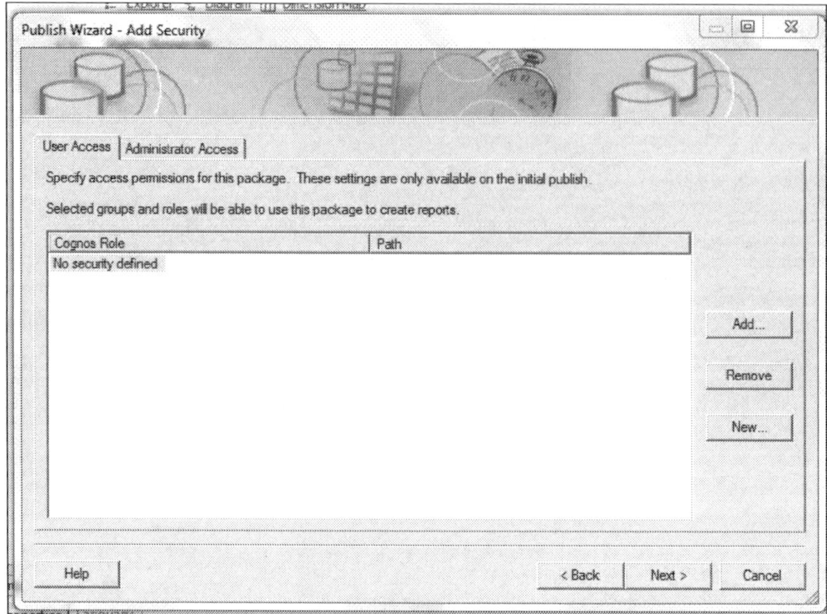

To add security click on the **Add** button. This will show the following dialog:

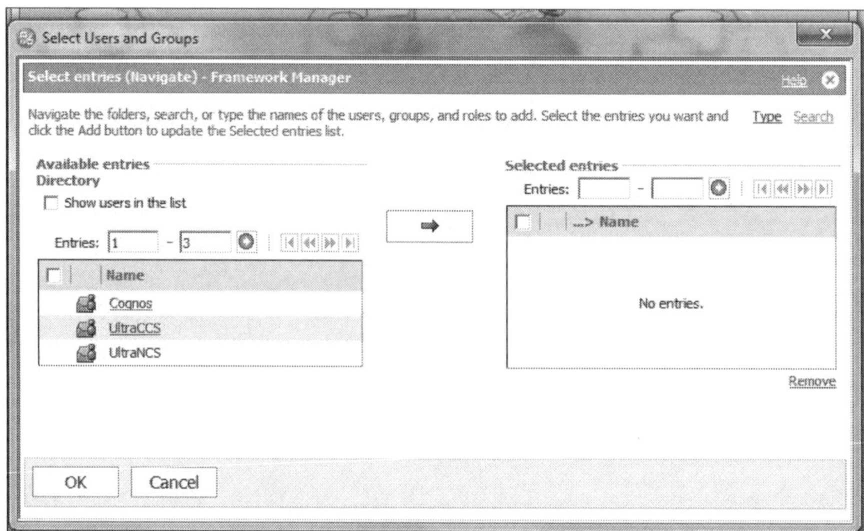

Expand the available entries and select the appropriate security group or role.

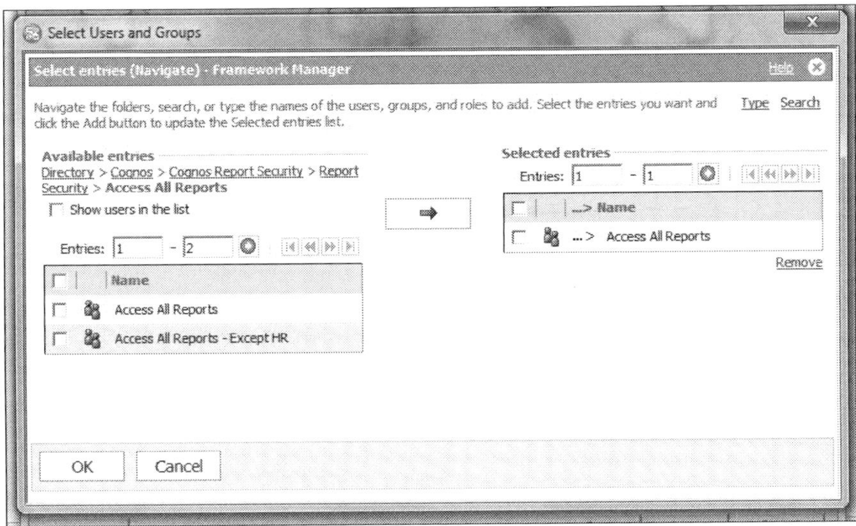

When the required security class has been selected click on the **OK** button to accept the choice.

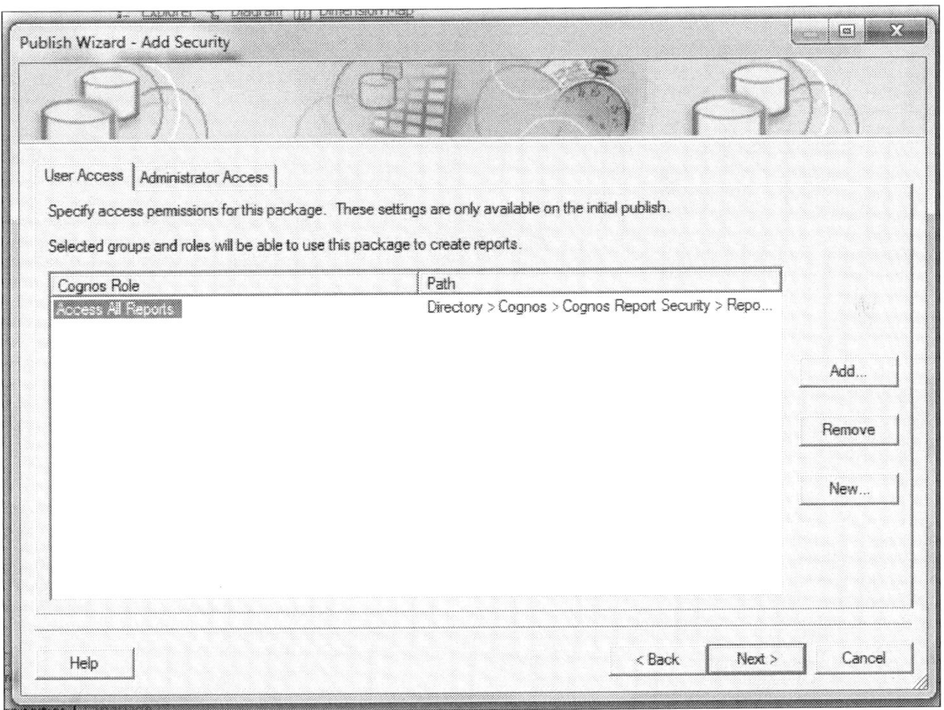

Apply the package security from within IBM Cognos Connection rather than during package creation/publication, since this is where the security will be maintained after the package is first published.

Summary

In this chapter, we have looked at creating packages for our reporting metadata to make this available for the report authors. We have also looked at publishing the packages to the IBM Cognos Report Server.

In the next chapter, we will look at maintaining projects, and enabling your projects for multiple users.

8

Maintaining Projects

Framework Manager models are not static objects and once a model has been implemented it transitions into a maintenance mode characterized by the need for small changes over time. The underlying relational database may be changed by adding or removing columns from the tables, changing the data types of columns on the tables, or even changing the database vendor. These types of changes, and others, have to be reflected in the model through a managed change process. This chapter will cover some of the methods used to maintain these changes within the Framework Manager project.

We will also look at some of the methods available to allow multiple modelers to work with the same model.

This chapter will cover the following topics:

- Analyzing the impact of changes made to packages
- Finding report dependencies
- Showing item dependencies
- Remapping an item to a new source
- Branching and merging projects
- Segmenting and linking projects

By the end of this chapter you will be able to implement changes to the underlying data sources, and identify to report authors where changes will need to be made to their reports due to changes in packages created from the Framework Manager projects.

You will also be able to work with other modelers to make changes to the same Framework Manager projects.

Analyzing the impact of changes made to packages

Changes made to a project may impact reports already created using packages from the model, especially if query item names are changed or removed.

Adding new items to your model will not affect any existing reports that are based on packages from the model; however, if you rename or delete a query item from your model then any reports created using those items will no longer be valid because the query item is no longer part of the model package. Before republishing a package, you can see if any changes you have made to your model will affect any existing reports that use the package. You can find all of the changes that have been made to the package in the current session, as well as see details for each change and find out the names of reports affected by a specific change.

> If you do not publish any of the packages using your model then no reports will be affected by the changes.
>
> You can make use of package versions when publishing your package to minimize the impact on existing reports when you make any changes to your model. See *Chapter 7, Creating and Publishing Packages* for more information.

The analysis of your model will show changes to any of the following types of items in your Framework Manager project:

- Query subjects
- Query items
- Measures
- Dimensions
- Hierarchies
- Levels
- Stand-alone filters
- Stand-alone calculations

Analyzing publish impact

Framework Manager has a facility to analyze the impact of publishing your package on any existing reports:

1. From the **Project Viewer** pane, right-click on a package that has already been published.
2. From the pop-up menu, select **Package | Analyze Publish Impact**.
3. Choose whether you want to:
    - Show report dependencies
    - Show item dependencies

Showing report dependencies

You can find all the reports that use any item that you have changed or added to your model.

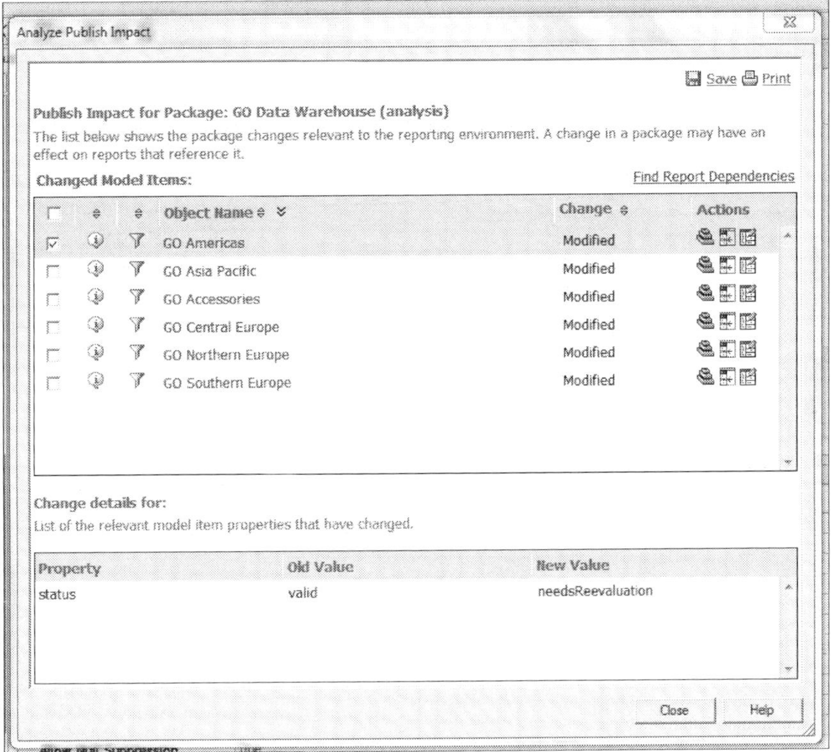

From the **Analyze Publish Impact** dialog box, do one of the following:

- Select the items you want to determine the report dependencies for by selecting the checkbox beside the item name
- Select all the items by selecting the checkbox at the top of the checkbox column
- Click on **Find Report Dependencies** label and do the following:
    1. Specify the scope of the search to use.
    2. To search all folders, click on **All Folders** or to search a specific folder click on **Restrict Search (Browse and select a folder)** and then type the name of the folder into the textbox or click on **Browse** and select the specific folder.

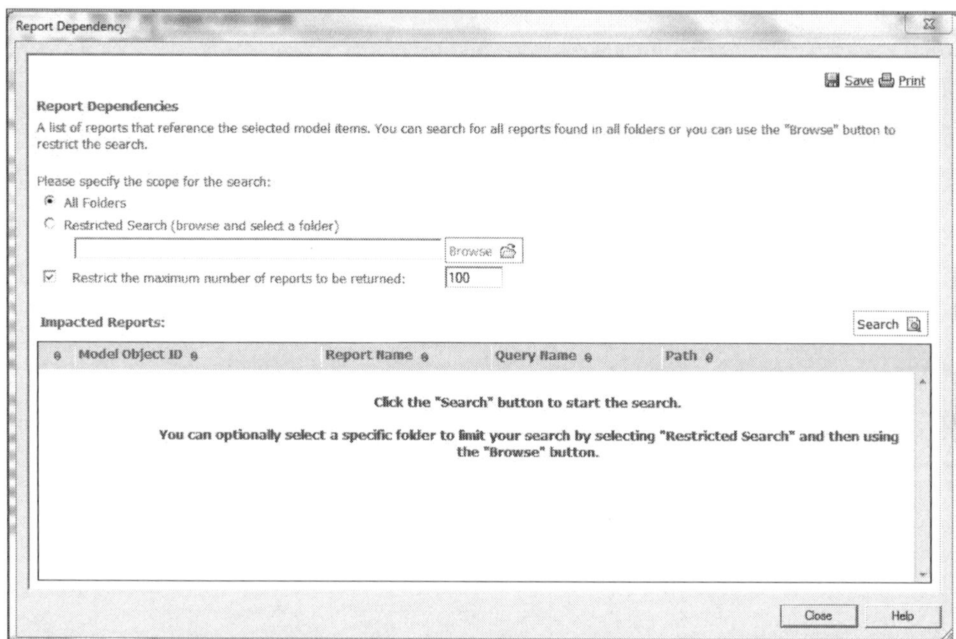

3. Click on **Search**, after a short delay a list of report names will show in the **Impacted Reports** panel of the **Report Dependency** window.

To print the list of reports so that they can be reviewed after the package is published, click on the **Print** label in the top-right corner of the **Report Dependency** window.

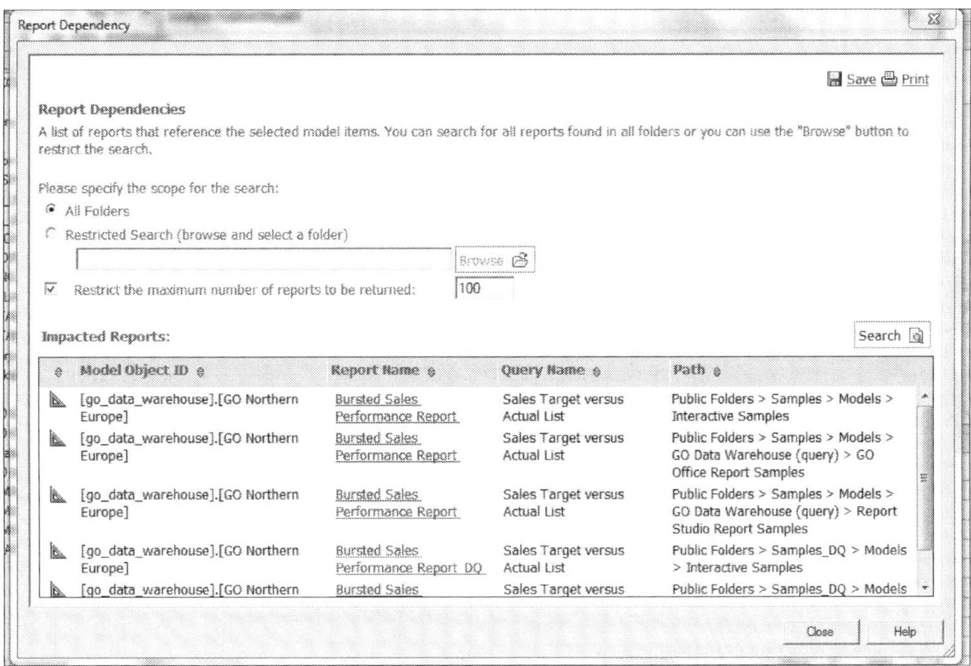

Showing item dependencies

You can also find any item that depends on other changed items in the model.

1. In the **Analyze Publish Impact** window, in the row for the item you are interested in, from the **Actions Items**, select **Show Dependencies**.

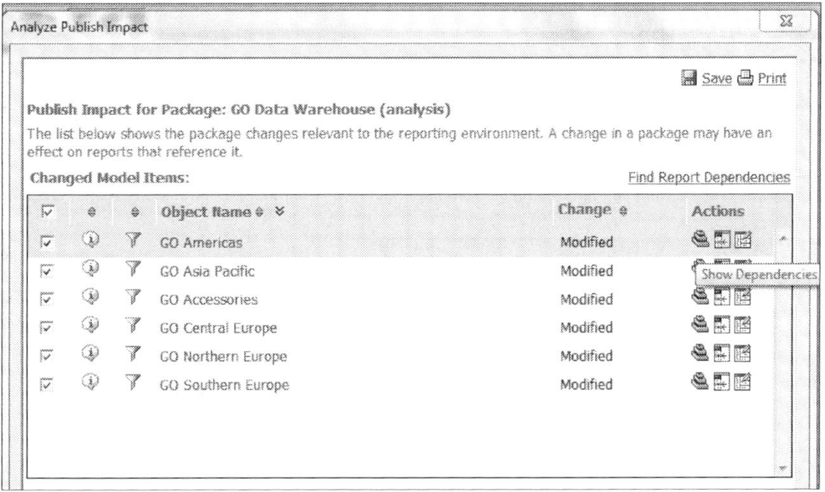

The selected item is copied to the **Dependencies** tab in the tools pane, and the dependent items appear in the **Dependent objects** panel as shown in the following screenshot:

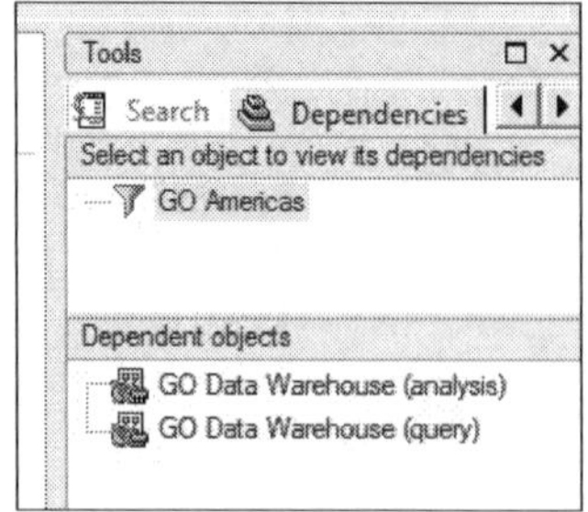

2. If the dependent item has children and you want to see the dependencies for the child items, click on the plus sign (+) beside the item.

[You can also show item dependencies by right-clicking on any item in **Project Viewer** and selecting **Show Item Dependencies** from the pop-up menu.]

Remapping an item to a new source

Over time you may want to make more radical changes to your Framework Manager model. You may, for example, want to change the model to replace an existing import view with a new import view, or use a different database with the same data.

You can reduce the impact of making changes to your data sources by remapping your model at the import layer of your model. When you remap items in your model you are replacing the original items with new items. You can remap single items or you can remap multiple items at the same time. When you remap multiple items, Framework Manager only matches and replaces those items that meet your chosen matching criteria; any other item will be ignored.

[If your report authors have already created reports then run **Analyze Publish Impact**, and use **Find Report Dependencies** to identify any affected reports when you remap any item in your model.]

How to remap an item

The procedure to remap an item is as follows:

1. In the **Project Viewer** window, right-click on an item and select **Remap To New Source**; you will see the following dialog:

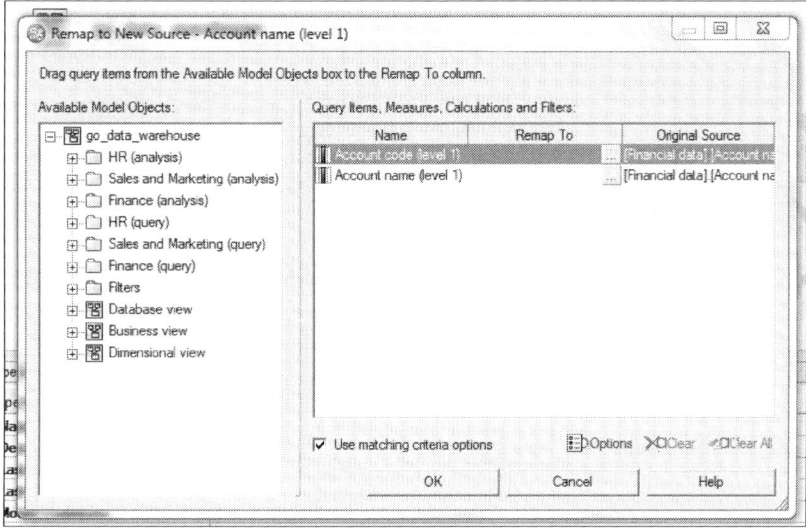

2. To change the matching criteria, click on **Options** and do the following:

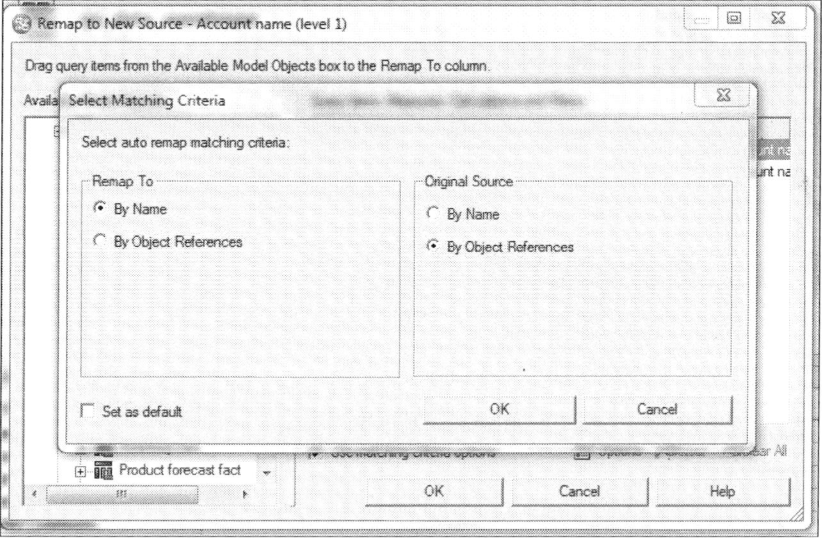

1. Choose the matching criteria for **Remap To** and **Original Source**.
2. You can match items by name or by object reference. Matching by name matches the object names, and matching by object reference matches using internal codes within Framework Manager.
3. Click on **OK**.
4. To use the criteria you specified, select the **Use matching criteria** checkbox.

If the matching criteria are **By Name** to **By Name**, spaces within the string are ignored.

3. Do one or more of the following:
   1. To remap an individual item manually, under **Available Model Objects**, drag an item to the item you want to remap.
   2. To remap multiple items automatically, under **Available Model Objects**, drag a query subject to any row under **Query Items, Measure, Calculations and filters**.
   3. Click on the ellipsis (**...**) button beside the item to change the expression of an item.
   4. If you change your mind about remapping items, right-click on the row that contains the item and select **Restore to Original Value** to restore a remapped value to the original source value.
   5. Click on the row that contains the item and click on **Clear** to clear the remapped value and the original value for the selected item.
   6. Click on **Clear All** to clear the remap value for all items.
4. Click on **OK** when you have finished your remapping.

Reusing a project

Sometimes you may want to use an existing model and reports with different data sources, which could be different accounts or schemas within a single database. For this process to work successfully, all of the database tables and columns used by the project must be identical across all the data sources.

It is possible to use multiple data source connections in a single data source to assist the migration of your Framework Model from one environment to another. If you have access to multiple data source connections in a single data source, when you open Framework Manager you will be prompted to select the data source connection to use for the project.

For example, you can use multiple data source connections to work with metadata from a development and a production data source. When you create your new Framework Manager project and add the data source you will be prompted for the data source connection to use, to select the development data source connection, and create and modify the items you want in the project. After testing to ensure that the project is correct, you can then close the current session, and reopen the Framework Manager project. You can now select the production data source connection. When your users select a package from the model they can then choose the data source connection they want to use in their report.

Multiple data source connections to the same data source need to be defined in IBM Cognos Connection; they cannot be defined in Framework Manager.

Model portability

Sometimes it is necessary to change your Framework Manager project to access data from a different database vendor, for example moving your database from Oracle to SQL Server.

There are several things that need to be considered when making such migrations. Unlike changing from one identical database to another on the same platform, it may not be sufficient to just change the data source connection information.

To move the model from one relational database to another, here are a few of the tasks you will need to carry out:

- Review the **Data Definition Language** (**DDL**) used by the different databases to check for the portability of physical names and data. Not all databases support the same data types or precision of data; some databases may have restrictions on the length of table names, or may require the table names to be in lower- or uppercase.
- If you have used any native SQL statements in your models you will need to check that any vendor specific syntax is changed or removed.

- You will need to check the use of vendor specific functions in your model since there may not be an equivalent vendor function in the new database.
- If you change the RDBMS you use, such as from Oracle to SQL Server, you will also need to change the type property for the data source in Framework Manager.
- You should check for reserved words, as each vendor has additional reserved words.

Once you have moved your data source from one database to another you should thoroughly test the new model.

Use Tools, Verify Selected Object, to verify all the items in your model.

Moving a model by using the log file

You can move your Framework Manager model from one environment to another by using the Framework Manager log file.

The log file is created the first time you save your project and exists until you delete the project. The log file, `log.xml`, is saved in the project folder with the other project files. Every action that has been run and saved in the project since the model was originally created is stored in this log file.

Within Framework Manager, you can view and play back any of the actions saved in the log file. Alternatively, you can use the command line Script Player, `BmtScriptPlayer`, to play back the actions in batch mode.

It is easy to use the log file to transfer your Framework Manager project from a development to a production (or any other) environment. You only need to make changes to your mode in the development environment, and when you want to move the model to your production environment you can use the log file to replay the actions to create the identical project in your production environment.

How to play back actions from a log file

It is possible to play back specific actions, or the complete log file.

You can use the log file to restore a corrupted project file. The log file is created when the project is first saved so it has all the actions from the start of the model. Start with an empty project file, and replay from the first saved action.

1. From the **Project** menu, click on **Run Script**.
2. Select the script you want, and click on **Open**.
3. If you want to review the details of an action, click on the action.
4. Set any starting point or stopping point that you want.
    - To set the starting point for running the script, select the script and then click on **Set the starting point**. You can do this at any time to skip an instruction or run instructions that have already been executed.
    - To set a stop point for the script, select the script and then click on **Set the stop point**.
    - You can stop the script to make a manual fix and then start it again.

To remove the stop point, click on **Remove the stop point**.

    - Using the toolbar buttons, choose the run action that you want.
5. When you are ready to start your script simply press the **Run** button.
6. When the script has completed successfully, you will be prompted to **Accept** or **Reject** all changes made to your model.

When you replay the action from the log file a backup of the original project is created in the project parent directory. If you decide to undo all the actions performed by the script, you can restore the project to its original state from this backup.

Running action logs in batch mode

The Script Player is a Windows command line utility that runs action logs in batches. The command line script player is called `BmtScriptPlayer`.

The installation location of the `BmtScriptPlayer.exe` is usually <Cognos_Installation_Location>\bin.

BmtScriptPlayer syntax

Use the following syntax to run the Script Player:

```
BmtScriptPlayer -m <projectname> -a <actionlogname>
```

`<projectname>` is the name of the project and `<actionlogname>` is the name of the action log.

For example:

```
BmtScriptPlayer -m goSales.cpf -a import.xml
```

Multiuser modeling in Framework Manager

You can implement multiuser modeling in Framework Manager in the following ways:

- **Using branching and merging**: When you use this method, each user has their own branch copy of either the entire project or a subset of the project, and can make changes to this branch without affecting other parts, or other users. The individual branches can later be merged back into the main project.
- **Using segmenting and linking**: Every user can use the same parts of the overall model, but it is important that each user only modifies specific parts of the project. The project is generally made from one or more segments which are linked together for the main project.

Branching and merging projects allows multiple modelers to work on the model at the same time, since each has its own separate branch model which has been created from an overall model. There is no limit to the number of branches that a model can have; it is also possible to create a branch from an existing branch. It is important when using branching to regularly merge the branches back into the main project since this will make it easier to resolve any conflicts during the merge process. Branches should always be merged back into the root project in the reverse order of creating them. Adding new items to a branch should not have any impact on other branches, but deleting items may affect other members and cause difficulties when merging the branches back into the root (or into other branches).

IBM Cognos recommends three main strategies for creating branches in a project. They are as follows:

- **Hub and spoke**: In this method, the root project is fully modeled and contains all items for every area of the model. This root project is then branched into separate functional areas where each one has its own publishing layer.
- **Functional area specific metadata**: In this method, there is very little or no common metadata within the project. Each functional area will develop its own model without reference to any other functional area. All the separate functional area models are then merged into a single large root project by a separate "master" modeler.
- **Distribution by layers**: The metadata in the project is organized as layers. The root project is a fully modeled import layer, which is branched to create a business layer; again this layer is fully modeled to branch a project.

You can create a branch in a project as follows:

1. Open the project that you want to branch.
2. From the **Project** menu, click on **Branch to**.
3. In **Project** name box, type a name for the project.
4. In the **Location** box, type the path to the folder where you want to store the branched version of the project.

Merge projects

You can merge a branch back into its root project as follows:

1. Open the project into which you want to merge a branch.
2. From the **Project** menu, click on **Merge from**.
3. In the **Select Project to Merge From** dialog box, click on the **Files of Type** list and click on **All Files** (`*.*`).

4. Locate the `log.xml` file for the branch to be merged, and click on **Open**.

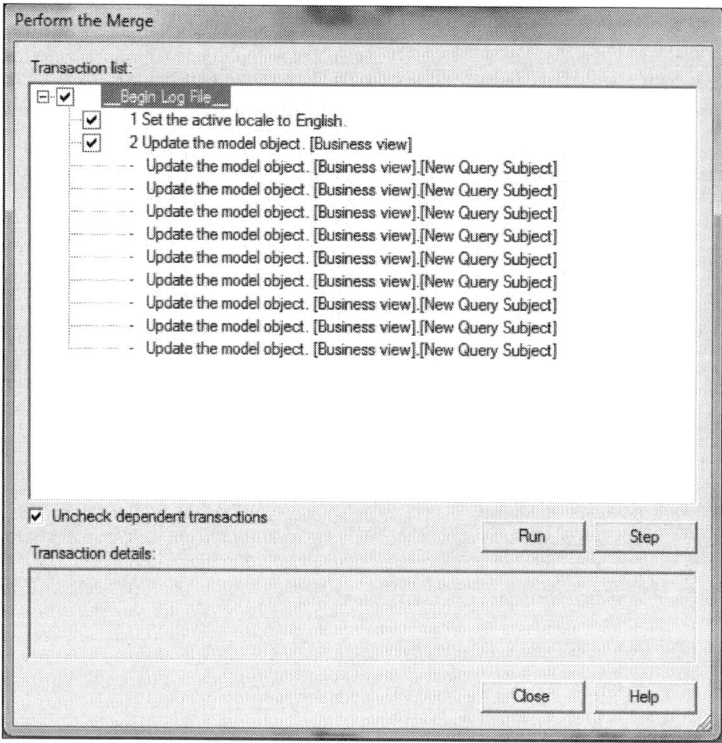

The **Perform the Merge** window opens, showing a list of actions.

5. Choose how to run the actions:
   - To run the entire action list continuously from start to finish, click on **Start**
   - To run one action and then pause, click on **Step**

When an action is completed, a check mark (**ü**) indicates that the action was applied successfully, while an **X** means that the action failed. If an action fails, the merge process will pause.

6. Choose one of the following actions:
   - **Fix**: Attempt to fix the error
   - **Skip**: Skip the action and continue after it
   - **Step**: Run the current action and pause

   - **Continue**: Run the current action until the end
   - **Accept**: Accept all actions up to the current action
   - **Revert**: Revert all actions

7. Perform the previous step until you reach the end of the action list or you have accepted or reverted the changes.
8. If you accepted the changes, save the merged project in the project folder. If you decide not to save the changes, close the project without saving it.

Segmenting and linking projects

Using segmenting and linking projects components can be created and shared between different models. It is only necessary to create the components once, the components can then be segmented, and linked to other projects when required.

Each project segment is a complete project and changes to the project will affect all projects to which the segment is linked.

Do not change the import layer in a segment. Any change will be reflected in the linked parent model and will impact all model segments that share data source query subjects. Changes may not be apparent until the model is closed and reopened.

Before a project is segmented it is important to ensure that the folder and namespace are named correctly, since once you have created the segment it is not possible to rename either the segment or the namespace.

The main project has access to the entire model, including the segments. You can make changes to any of the segments when working in the main project.

If you have a main project that contains segments it is possible to make changes to the entire model, including any segments that are linked by making changes to the main project.

Creating a segment

With segments, you can organize a project according to business rules or organizational requirements, and share and reuse project information.

You create segments at the folder level or the namespace level. You can create a new project in a new folder, complete with its own associated project files.

1. Click on the folder or namespace you want to divide, and from the **Project** menu, click on **Create Segment**.

Accept the default settings for the project name.

2. To rename the segment, in the **Project Name** box, type a different name.

This does not change the folder name. If you want to rename the folder, you should rename it in **Project Viewer** before creating the segment.

For ease of use, keep the same name for both the folder and the segment.

3. Click on **OK**.

Creating links

You create links to help organize work across large projects, and to reuse information.

1. In the **Project Viewer** window, click on the project, segment, namespace, or folder that you want to link to.

You can create links only to folders, namespaces, projects, or segments.

2. From the **Project** menu, click on **Link Segment**.
3. Locate and click on the `.cpf` file of the project that contains the item that you want to link to.
4. Click on **Open**.

If the project uses a mapped drive letter, you are prompted to keep the mapped drive letter or to change it to a UNC path. UNC paths will be better to use than mapped drives since not all users may have the same mapped drives.

5. Choose the project, segment, namespace, or folder to link to.
6. Click on **OK**.
7. A new folder appears in the **Project Viewer** window.

Summary

In this chapter, we have looked at managing your project when the data source or items in the model change. We have looked at how you can find out what effect any change made to the model will have on any report that makes use of packages published from the model.

We have also looked at the techniques available for multiuser modeling, allowing more than one person to work on a Framework Manager model simultaneously.

In the next chapter, we will look at the Model Design Accelerator. This is a new feature added to IBM Cognos Framework Manager which is designed to make it quicker to create a new Framework Manager model.

9
Model Design Accelerator

Model Design Accelerator is an extension of Framework Manager which has been designed to simplify the design and creation of a single fact relational star schema model. Model Design Accelerator can be used to create a relational star schema model that adheres to proven modeling practice. By using Model Design Accelerator, a novice modeler can build a Framework Manager model without extensive training, and a more experienced modeler can quickly build a new model, thereby reducing the time taken to design and build a Framework Manager model.

This chapter covers the following topics:

- The Model Design Accelerator user interface
- Starting Model Design Accelerator
- Adding tables
- Adding joins
- Generating Framework Manager models

By the end of this chapter you will be able to use Model Design Accelerator to design a new Framework model.

To introduce Model Design Accelerator, we will use a fairly simple schema based on a rental star schema, derived from the MySQL `Sakila` sample database. This database can be downloaded from `http://dev.mysql.com/doc/sakila/en/`. It is just one example of a number of possible dimensional models based on this sample database. The schema for this sample database can be found in *Appendix, Data Warehouse Schema Map*. To use this schema, you will need to create a data source connection to the database before starting.

Model Design Accelerator user interface

The user interface of Model Design Accelerator is very simple, consisting of only two panels:

- **Explorer Tree**: This contains details of the database tables and views from the data source.
- **Model Accelerator**: This contains a single fact table surrounded by four dimension tables, and is the main work area for the model being designed.

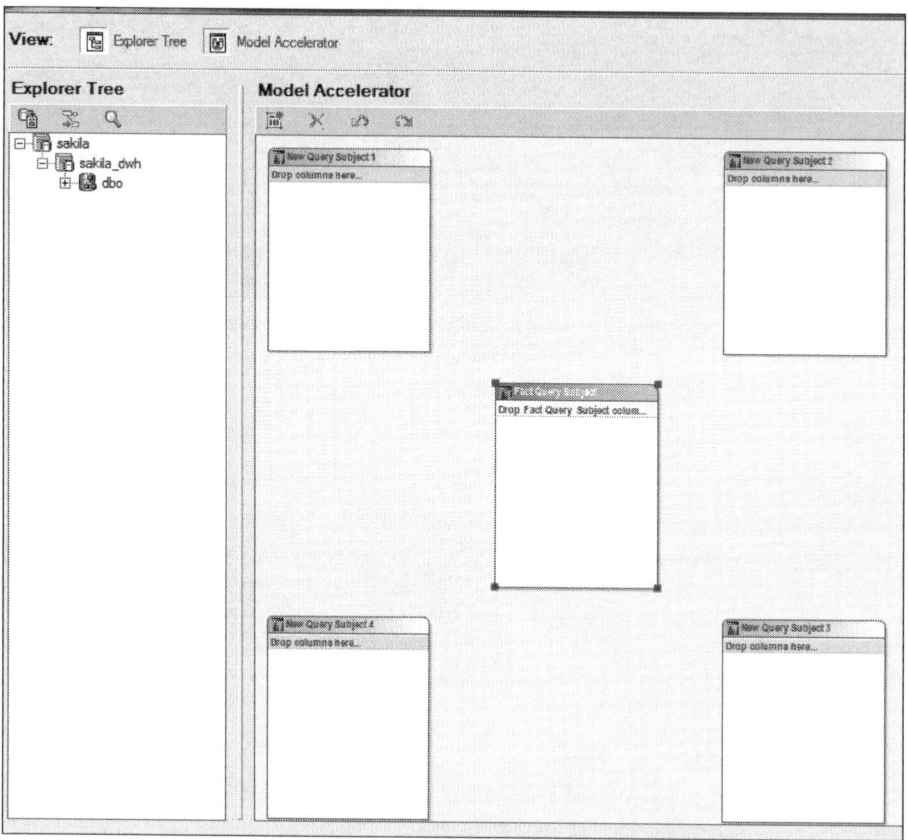

By clicking on the labels (**Explorer Tree** and **Model Accelerator**) at the top of the window, it is possible to hide either of these panels, but having both these panels always visible is beneficial.

Starting Model Design Accelerator

Model Design Accelerator is started from the Framework Manager initial screen:

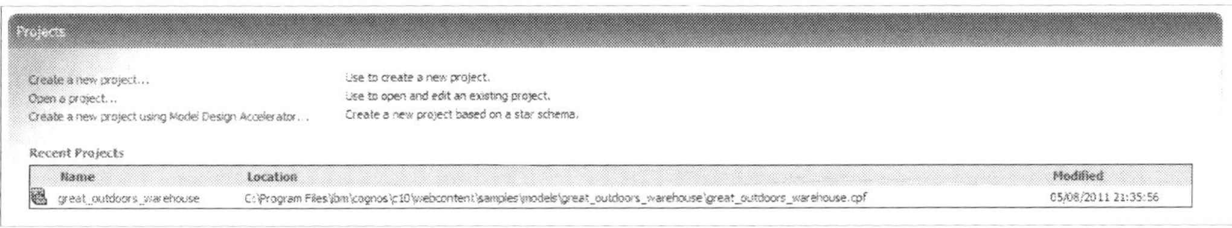

1. Select **Create a new project using Model Design Accelerator...**.

   This will start the new project creation wizard, which is exactly the same as if you were starting any new project.

2. Select the data source to import the database tables into the new model. After importing the database tables, the project creation wizard will display the **Model Design Accelerator Introduction** screen:

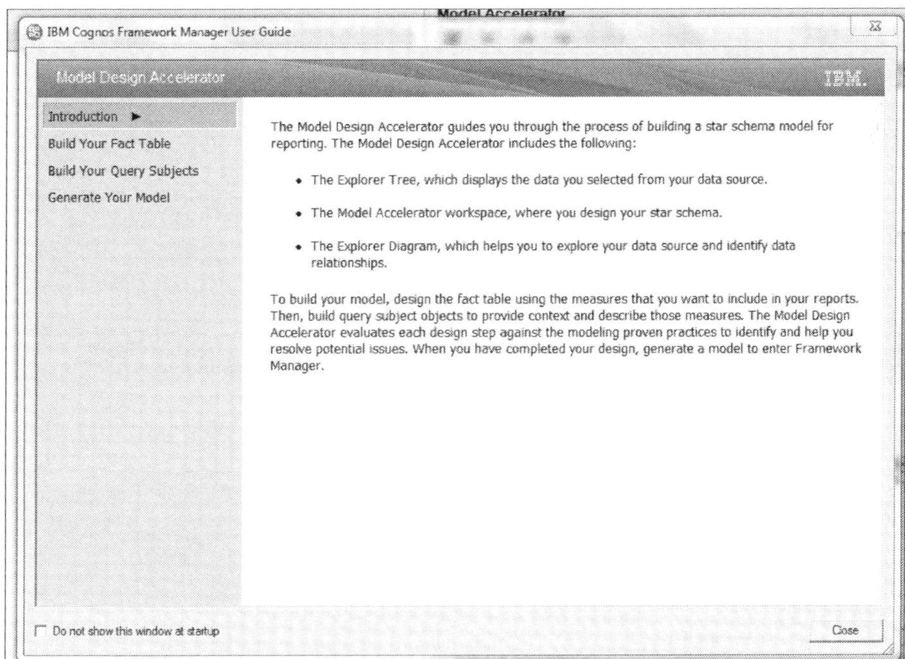

3. After reading the instructions, click on the **Close** button to continue.
4. This will then show the Model Design Accelerator workspace.

Adding tables to your workspace

The first step in creating your model with Model Design Accelerator is to add the dimension and fact tables to your model:

1. From the **Explorer** panel, drag-and-drop `dim_date`, `dim_film`, `dim_customer`, and `dim_store` to the four **New Query Subject** boxes in the **Model Accelerator** panel.
2. After adding your queries, right-click on the boxes to rename the queries to `Rental Date Dim`, `Film Dim`, `Customer Dim`, and `Store Dim` respectively.

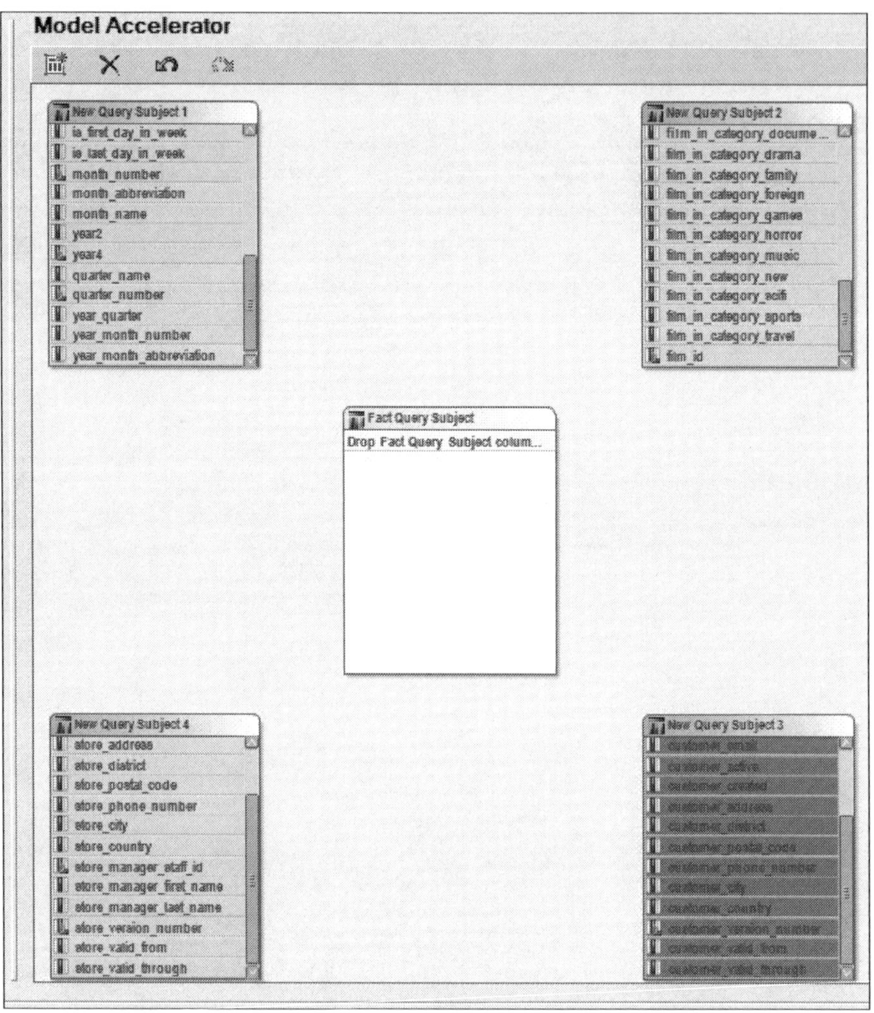

If not all query columns are required, it is also possible to expand the dimension tables and drag-and-drop individual columns to the query boxes.

3. In the **Explorer Tree** panel, expand the `fact_rental` table by clicking on the (+) sign besides the name, and from the expanded tree drag-and-drop `count_returns`, `count_rentals`, and `rental_duration` columns to the **Fact Query Subject** box.
4. Rename the **Fact Query Subject** to `Rental Fact`.
5. Additional dimension queries can be added to the model by clicking on the top-left icon in the **Model Accelerator** panel, and then by dragging and dropping the required query onto the workplace window.
6. Since we have a `start_date` and an `end_date` for the rental period, add a second copy of the `date_dim` table, by clicking on the icon and dragging the table from the **Explorer view** into the workspace. Also rename this query as `Return Date Dim`:

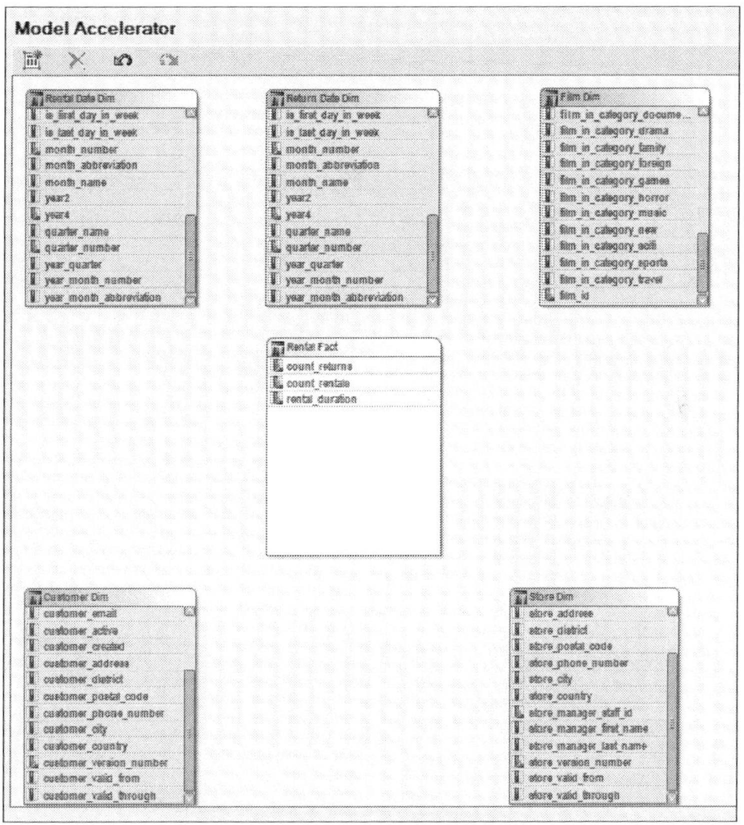

Adding joins to your workspace

After we have added our database table columns to the workspace, we now need to add the relationship joins between the dimension and fact tables. To do this:

1. Double-click on the `Rental Date Dim` table, and this will expand the `date_dim` and the `fact_rental` tables in the workspace window:

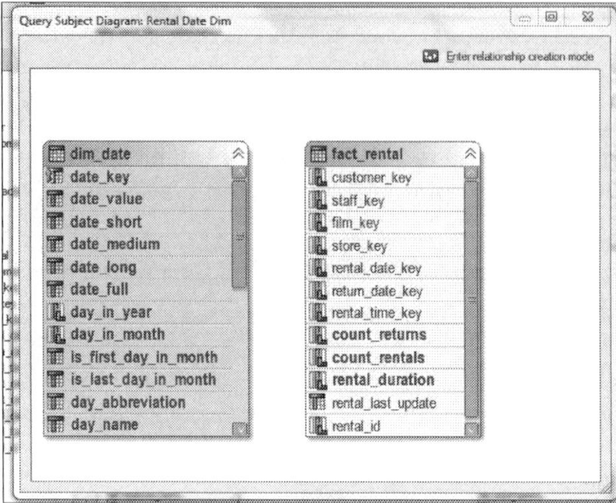

2. Click on the **Enter relationship creation mode** link.
3. Select the `date_key` column in the `dim_date` table, and the `rental_date_key` column in the `fact_rental` table as follows:

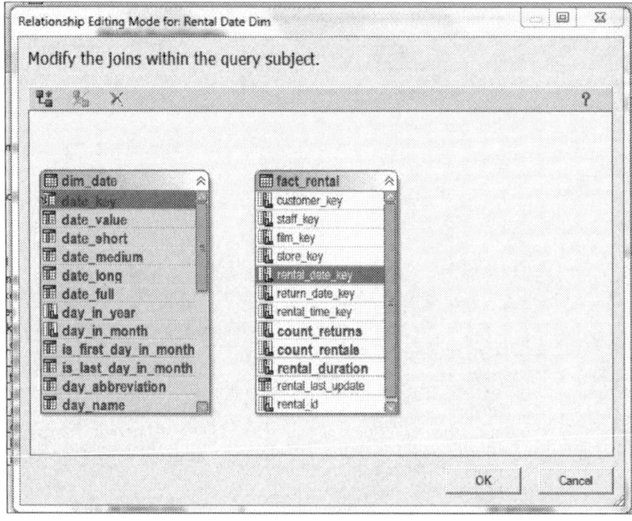

4. Click on the **Create relationship** icon:

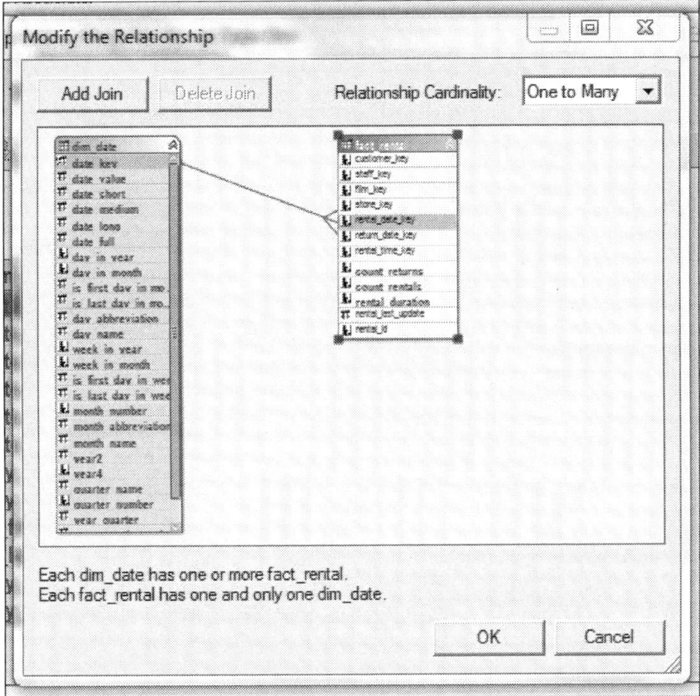

5. Click on **OK** to create this join.
6. Close the Query Subject Diagram by clicking on the (**X**) symbol in the top-right corner.
7. Repeat this procedure for each of the other four tables; the details of the joins to use can be found in *Appendix, Data Warehouse Schema Map*.

The final model will look like the following screenshot:

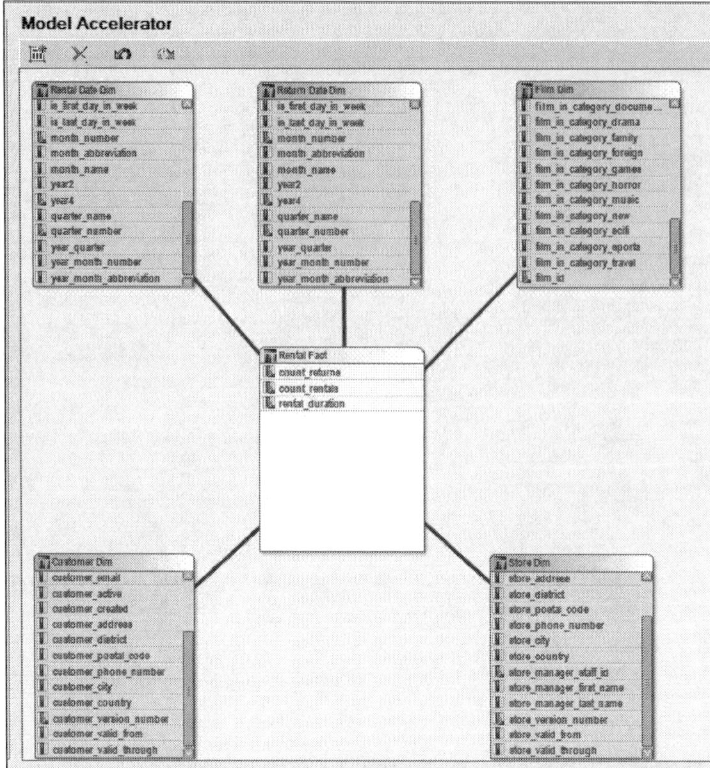

Generating a Framework Manager model

Once we have completed our model in Model Design Accelerator, we need to create a Framework Manager model:

1. Click on the **Generate Model** button.
2. Click on **Yes** to generate your model.

   The Framework Manager model will be generated and will open as follows:

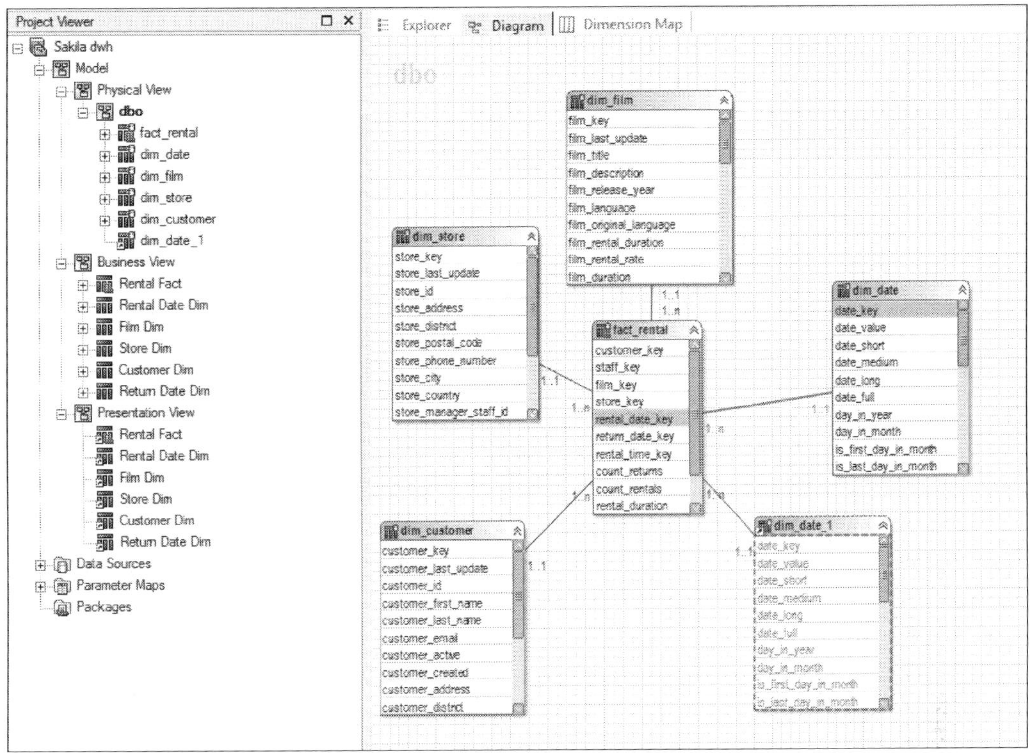

When you generate your model, all of the Model Advisor tests are automatically applied to the resulting model. You should review any issues that have been identified in the **Verify Results** tab, and decide whether you need to fix them.

When you generate the model only those query items required will be used to create the Framework Manager model. The **Physical View** tab will contain only those tables required by your star schema model. The **Business View** tab will contain model query subjects containing only the columns used in your star schema model. The **Presentation View** tab will only contain shortcuts to the query subjects that exist in the **Business View** tab.

After generating your model, you can use Framework Manager to improve the model by adding calculations, filters, dimensions, measures, and so on.

Each time you generate a Framework Manager model from your Model Design Accelerator model, a new namespace is created in the current Framework Manager model and any improvements you want to use will also need to be applied to these new namespaces.

From Framework Manager you can return to Model Design Accelerator at any time to continue making changes to your star schema.

To return to the Model Design Accelerator from within Framework Manager:

1. From the **Tools** menu, select **Run Model Design Accelerator**.
2. You may choose to continue with the same model or create a new model.

To make your star schema model available to the report authors, you must first create a package and then publish the package to your Cognos Reporting Server.

Summary

In this chapter, we have looked at Model Design Accelerator. This is a tool that allows a novice modeler, or even an experienced modeler, to create a new Framework Manger model quickly and easily.

In the next chapter, we will look at the use of parameter maps to include additional dynamic content into our Framework model.

10
Parameter Maps

This chapter introduces session parameters and parameter maps, both of which can be used to customize reports. Session parameters are values pulled from the user session. Parameter maps can be thought of as simple data look-up tables. Each parameter map has two columns, a key column and a value column holding the value that the key represents. A parameter map can be used to create a conditional query that allows for substitutions when a report is run. The following topics will be covered in this chapter:

- Creating and using session parameters
- Creating and using parameter maps

By the end of this chapter, you will understand how session parameters and parameter maps can be created and used within Framework Manager.

Session parameters

Every Framework Manager model has a set of built-in parameters that contain values related to the current session. These session parameters can be used by modelers in filters, calculations, and on reports.

The default session parameters include the following:

- `account.defaultName`: This returns the name of the current user as defined in the authentication provider, and examples of the values returned are the user's first and last name.
- `account.personalInfo.userName`: This returns the user ID used to log on to IBM Cognos BI if the user is logged in as Anonymous then this is not set.

- `runLocale`: This returns a code for the current active language in Framework Manager, and examples of the values returned by this parameter are en-gb, en-us, zh-cn, and zh-tw, which indicate English (United Kingdom), English(United States), Chinese(Simplified), and Chinese(Traditional) respectively.
- `current_timestamp`: This returns the current date and time.
- `machine`: This returns the name of the computer where Framework Manager is installed.

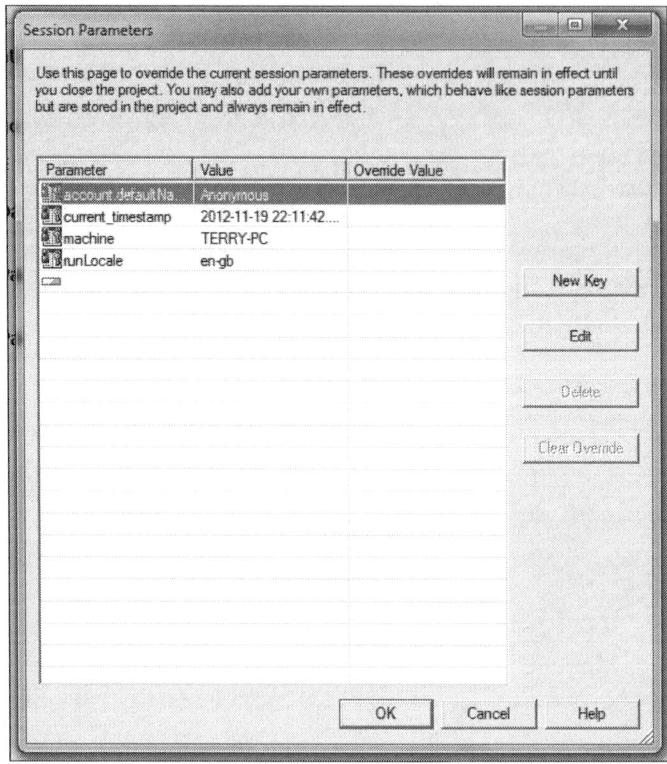

Some authentication sources support other parameters and if information about them has been entered, you may also see other session parameters. Common session parameters that you may see include `account.personalInfo.email`, `account.personalInfo.firstname`, and `account.personalInfo.surname`.

Additional parameters can be defined by using model session parameters. The model session parameters are always stored in a map named `_env`, and because they are set within the project they can be published with any packages.

Every session parameter created in the model must have a unique name and a default value. An override value can also be defined to allow the session value to be tested. If an override value is provided, it is not saved with the model and is only valid until the model is closed. Framework Manager will always use the default value when executing any query containing the session parameter if an override value is not set.

There are two important rules governing the use of session parameters:

1. All session parameters must return values of the same data type.
2. A key must only return a single value.

Creating a session parameter

Creating session parameters takes a few simple steps:

1. From the **Project** menu, click on **Session Parameters**.
2. Click on **New Key** and type a session parameter and its value:

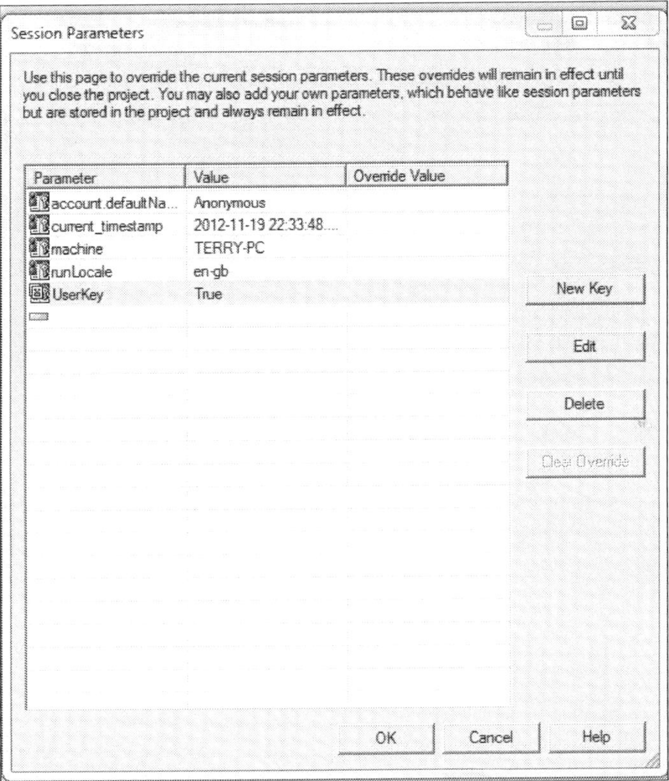

3. You can set the session parameter value to avoid setting the override value each time you edit the project, or you can also set the session parameter override value to avoid removing the parameter setting before you publish your package.

You cannot alter the default value of session parameters; you can only set an override value for any of them.

4. Click on **OK** to save your changes.

Modifying session parameters

You can modify the session parameters in a way similar to setting session parameters:

1. From the **Project** menu, click on **Session Parameters**.
2. To change a parameter value, click on the row that contains the value you want to change, and click on **Edit** to type a new value.
3. To assign a default value in the **Default Value** box, type a value. Framework Manager will use the default value if a key has an invalid value.
4. To remove a parameter, click on a row and then click on the **Delete** button.
5. To clear an override value, click on a row and then click on **Clear Override**.

Using session parameters

When you add a session parameter to your data source query subject you need to assign an alias to the parameterized object, and this ensures that the object returns the correct results when the parameter value changes.

The following SQL example defines a data source query containing the session parameter named `runLocale`. The `runLocale` parameter value is used to specify which column the query retrieves. The alias behaves like a shortcut so that when a model object references the alias, Framework Manager will retrieve the value to which the alias is assigned:

```
Select
  #$ColumnMap{$runLocale}# as CountryNameAlias
From
  [GoSales].Country
```

If the `runLocale` parameter returns the `en` value, then this will translate the SQL statement into the following code:

```
Select
  Countryen as CountryNameAlias
From [Goales].Country
```

It is often desirable to include the name of the user who has run a report. To do this, you can create a calculated item containing the following:

```
#sq ( $account.defaultName ) #
```

This will return the value of the `account.defaultName` session parameter, surrounded by single quote (') characters. With this calculated item available in your package your report authors can simply add it to their reports to display the login name of the user running the report.

Parameter maps

When we looked at session parameters, we have seen that although they are useful they are very limited and each time we want to use a session parameter to return a particular value, we have to edit the session parameter to either add a default value or an override value. If we want to create a session parameter that can return different values for different keys, then we create a parameter map.

Parameter maps can be thought of as simple data look-up tables. Each parameter map has two columns, a key column and a value column holding the value that the key represents. You can enter the keys and values manually, import them from an external file, or base them on query items in the model.

It is possible to export parameter maps to a file and to import parameter maps from a file. This is particularly useful if you have a large or complex parameter map. You can export the parameter map values to a file, make changes, and then import the modified parameter map back into Framework Manager.

There is one very important rule for all parameter maps:

- All parameter map keys must be unique so that the Framework Manager can reliably obtain the correct value

The value of one parameter can be the value of another parameter, so you must enclose the entire value in number signs (#). There is a limit of five levels when nesting parameters in this way.

How to create parameter maps

There are two ways to create a new parameter map in your Framework model:

1. Manually.
2. Basing it on a query item.

Creating a parameter map manually

You can enter the parameter map keys and values from the keyboard or read them in from a file.

1. Click on the `Parameter Maps` folder and from the **Actions** menu, navigate to **Create | Parameter Map**:

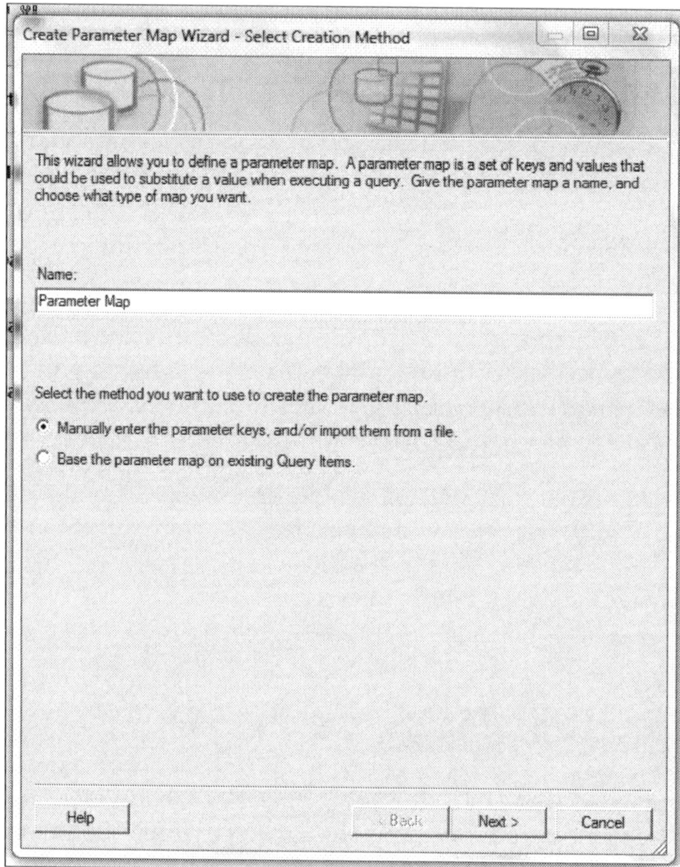

2. In the **Name** box, type a name for the new parameter map.
3. Select **Manually enter the parameter keys**, and/or import them from a file and then click on **Next**:

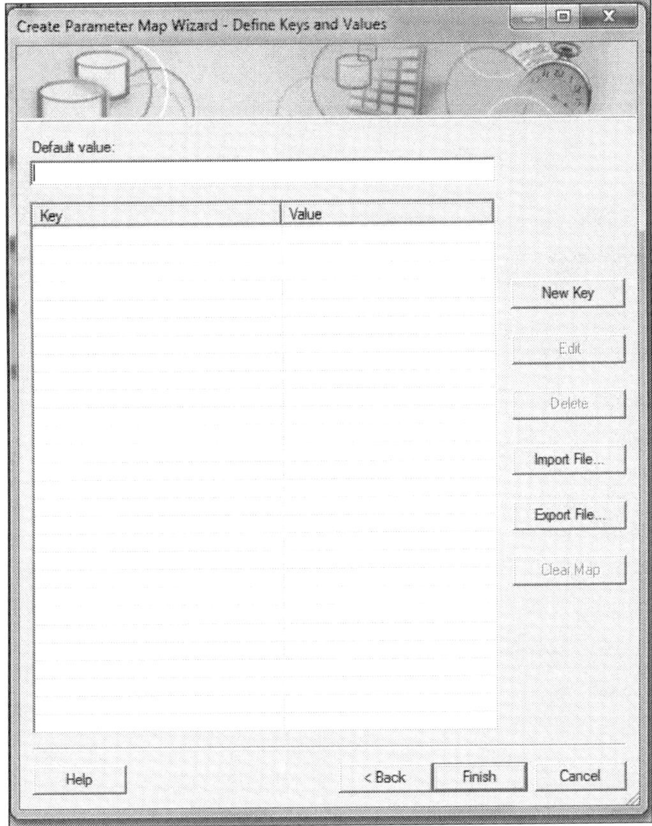

4. To manually enter values, click on **New Key**, and type a key name. Press the *Tab* key to enter a value for that key.
5. To import keys and values, click on **Import File** and identify the location of a `.csv` or `.txt` file.

> To use a `.txt` file for import, the values must be separated by tabs and the file must be saved as `UTF8` or in the `Unicode` format. `ANSI` text files are not supported.

6. Modify the values as required.

7. To assign a default value, type a value in the **Default Value** box.
   - To remove a parameter, select the row to be deleted and click on **Delete**.
   - To modify a parameter, select the row you want to modify, and click on the **Edit** button to type a new value.
   - To clear all keys and values, click on **Clear Map**.
8. Click on **Finish**.

Basing a parameter map on existing query items

You can create your parameter map from a query item as follows:

1. Click on the `Parameter Maps` folder and from the **Actions** menu, navigate to **Create | Parameter Map**.
2. In the **Name** box, type a name for the new parameter map.
3. Select **Base the parameter map on existing Query Items** and click on **Next**:

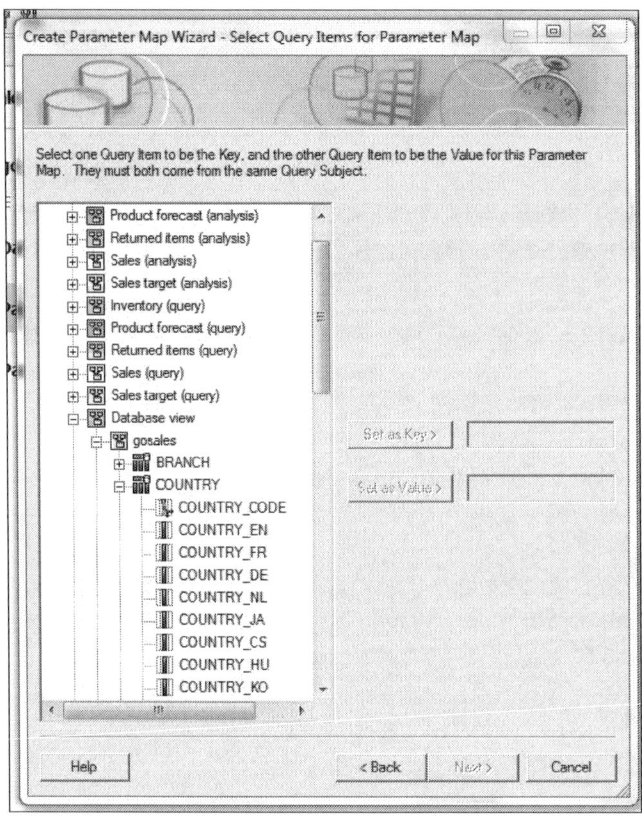

4. Click on the query item to be used as the key, and then click on the query item to be used as the value:

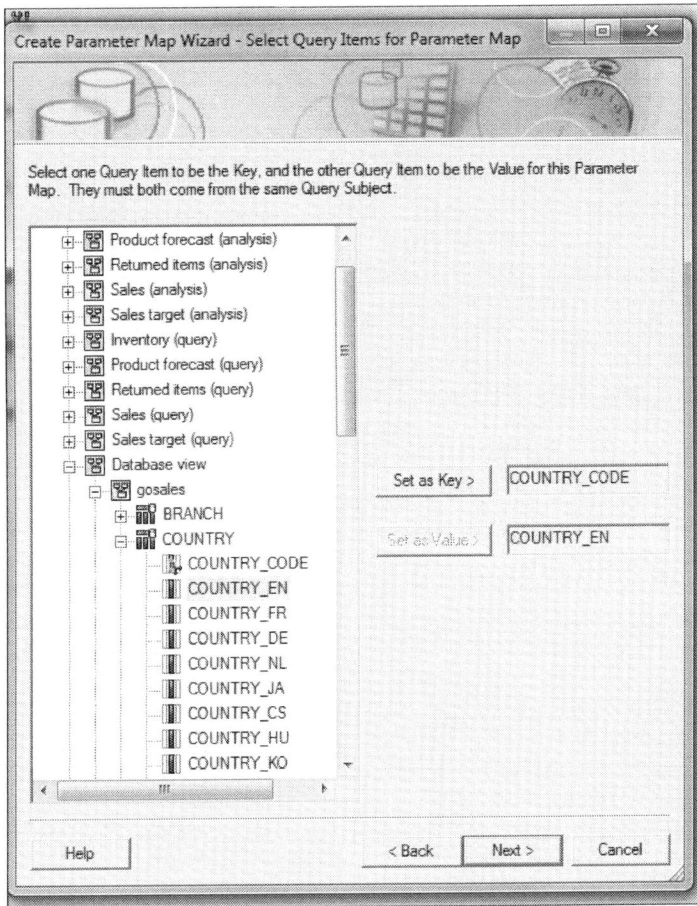

Both query items must be from the same query subject.

5. Click on **Next**:

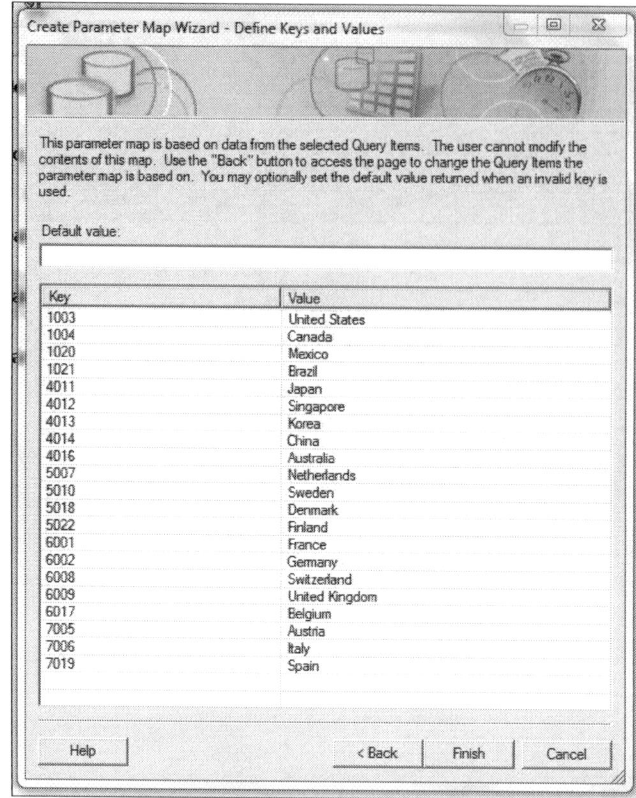

6. In the search box, type a value.

   The default value is used if the key is not mapped, because an unmapped key would otherwise produce an error.

7. Click on the **Finish** button.

Using parameter maps

To illustrate the use of parameter maps we will use the Great Outdoor Sales model supplied with the Cognos Samples.

This model has a parameter map called **Language_lookup** as shown in the following screenshot:

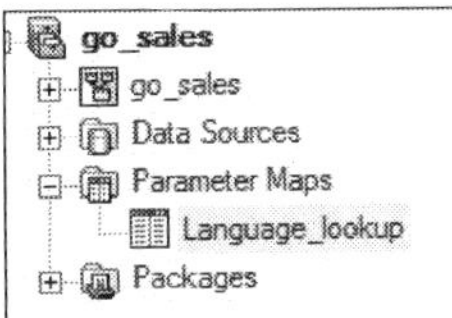

1. Double-click on the parameter map to open it so that we can review the contents:

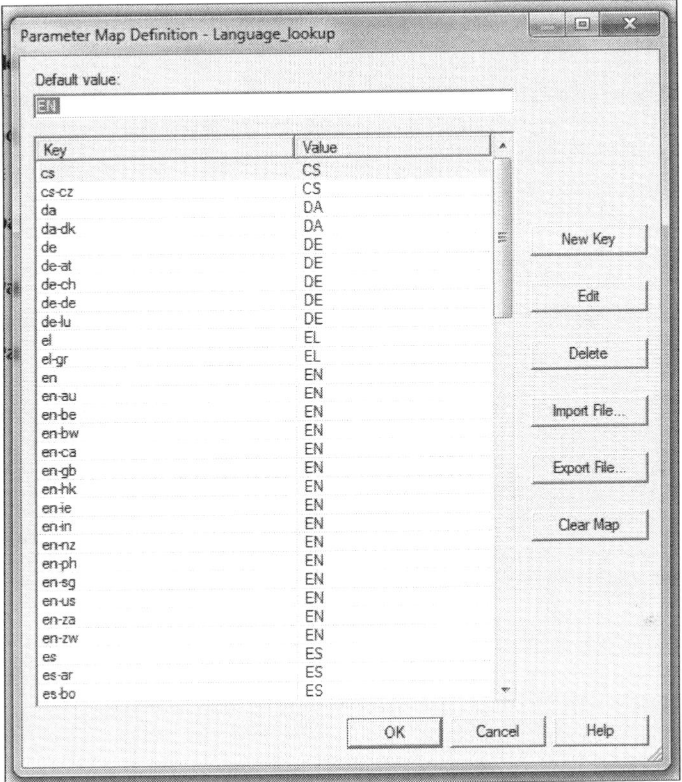

This parameter map maps the `runLocale` session parameter onto a value. If the value does not exist in the parameter map then it will return a default value of **EN**.

2. Click on **Cancel** to close the dialog box. Create a new query item from the **Actions** menu and navigate to **Create | Query Subject**.
3. Name the query subject as `Product_Name_Lookup`:

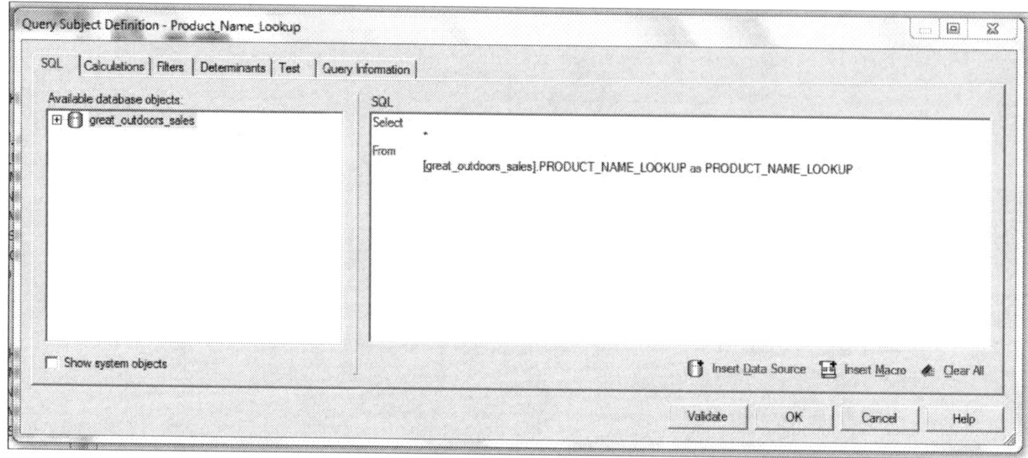

4. Click on the **Filters** tab and add a new filter:

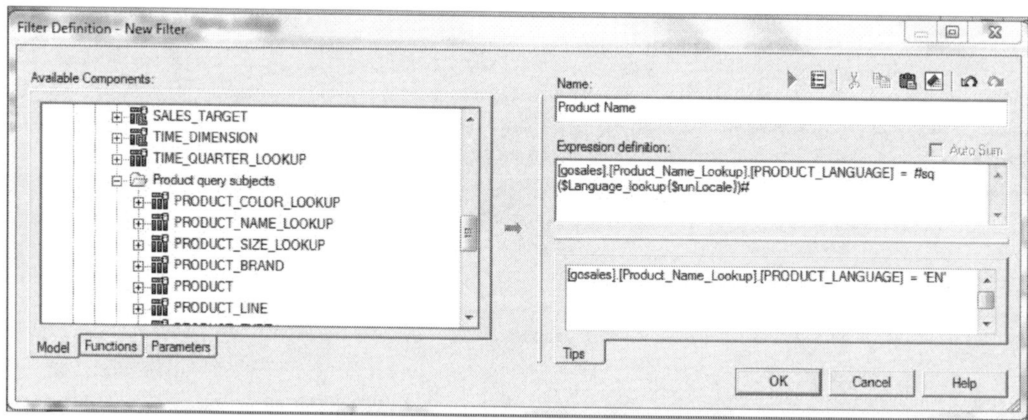

5. In the **Expression definition** box for the filter add the following:

```
[gosales].[Product_Name_Lookup].[PRODUCT_LANGUAGE]  =
#sq($Language_lookup{$runLocale})#
```

6. Test the query and examine the generated SQL:

```
SELECT "product_name_lookup"."product_number" AS "PRODUCT_NUMBER",
"product_name_lookup"."product_language" AS "PRODUCT_LANGUAGE",
"product_name_lookup"."product_name" AS "PRODUCT_NAME",
```

```
"product_name_lookup"."product_description" AS "PRODUCT_
DESCRIPTION"
FROM "GOSALES"."gosales"."product_name_lookup" "Product_Name_
Lookup"
WHERE "product_name_lookup"."product_language" = N'EN'
```

7. Navigate to **Project | Session Parameters**, and set **Override Value** for the `runLocale` session parameter to `fr` as follows:

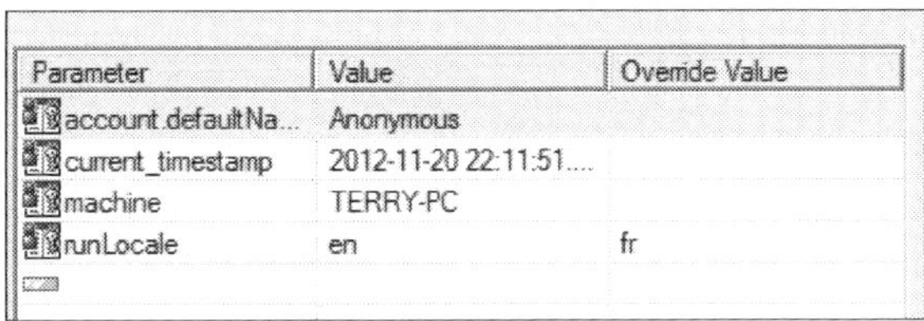

Parameter	Value	Override Value
account.defaultNa...	Anonymous	
current_timestamp	2012-11-20 22:11:51....	
machine	TERRY-PC	
runLocale	en	fr

8. Test the query once again, and examine the generated SQL:

```
SELECT "product_name_lookup"."product_number" AS "PRODUCT_NUMBER",
"product_name_lookup"."product_language" AS "PRODUCT_LANGUAGE",
"product_name_lookup"."product_name" AS "PRODUCT_NAME",
"product_name_lookup"."product_description" AS "PRODUCT_
DESCRIPTION"
FROM "GOSALES"."gosales"."product_name_lookup" "Product_Name_
Lookup"
WHERE "product_name_lookup"."product_language" = N'FR'
```

As can be seen in the previous code, by changing the `runLocale` session parameter value from `en` to `fr` we have changed the language used in the query from English to French.

Summary

In this chapter, we learned about session parameters and parameter maps as a way of changing the behaviour of the queries in your Framework Manager model. By using session parameters we made the creation of multi-lingual reports easier for our report authors. This is just one aspect of using session parameters and parameter maps. There are many other ways these can be applied, including on things such as setting the security within the model.

We also looked at the user interface for Framework Manager, and the best practice for using the software. We developed a model by using the best practices from importing our data source to refining our model, to produce a final package for our report authors. We looked at some additional features for further improving our model and some new features for making model development easier.

Data Warehouse Schema Map

This is the Schema Map for the Data Warehouse used in *Chapter 9, Model Design Accelerator*:

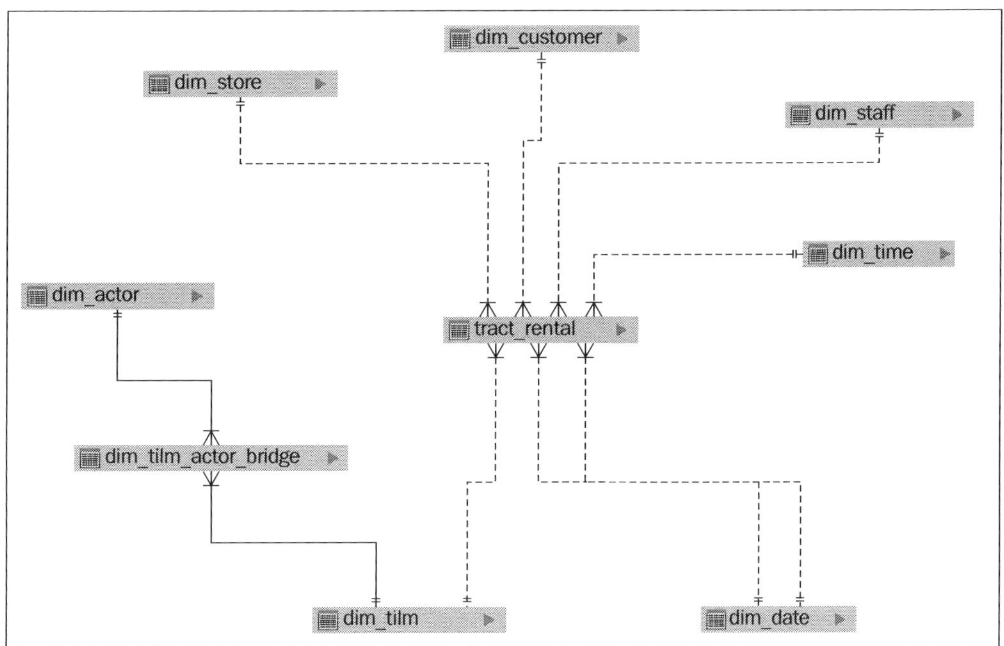

Table definitions

The following are the table definitions for the schema:

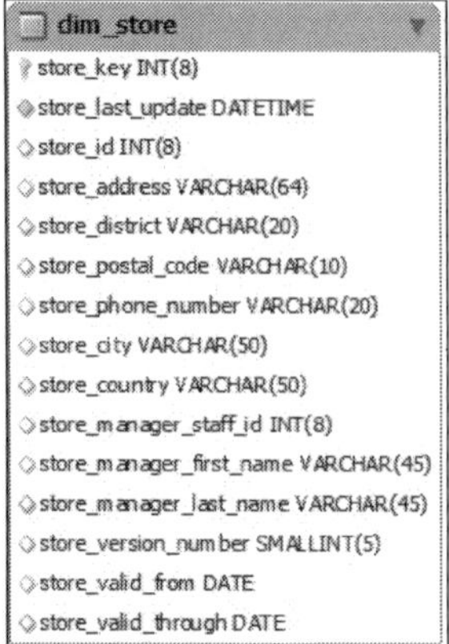

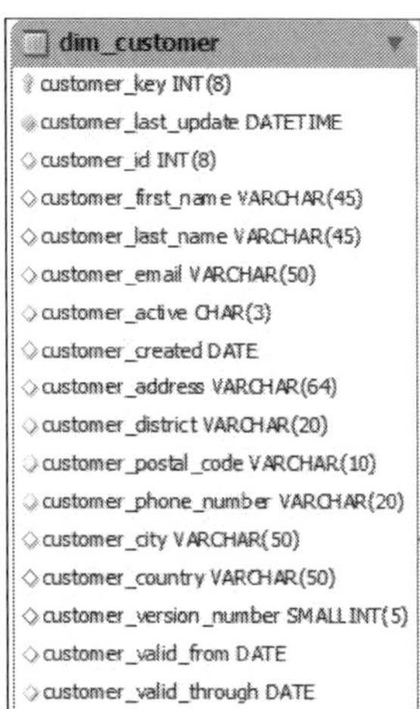

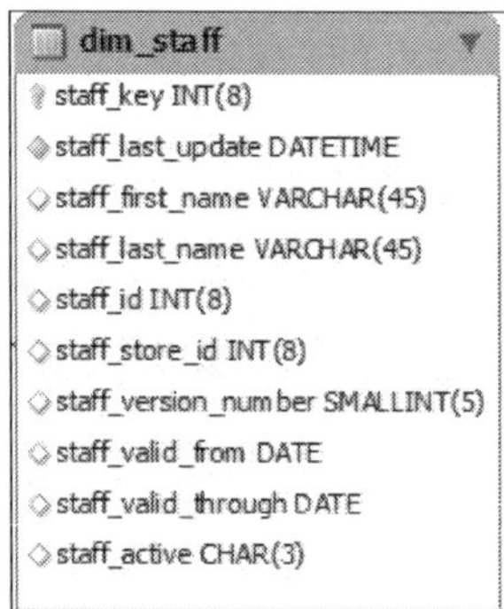

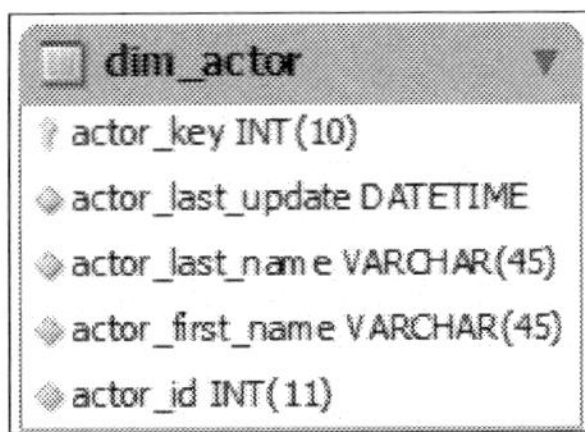
dim_actor
actor_key INT(10)
actor_last_update DATETIME
actor_last_name VARCHAR(45)
actor_first_name VARCHAR(45)
actor_id INT(11)

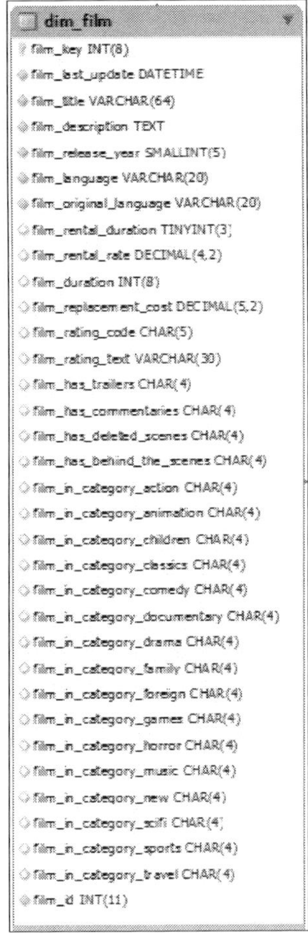
dim_film
film_key INT(8)
film_last_update DATETIME
film_title VARCHAR(64)
film_description TEXT
film_release_year SMALLINT(5)
film_language VARCHAR(20)
film_original_language VARCHAR(20)
film_rental_duration TINYINT(3)
film_rental_rate DECIMAL(4,2)
film_duration INT(8)
film_replacement_cost DECIMAL(5,2)
film_rating_code CHAR(5)
film_rating_text VARCHAR(30)
film_has_trailers CHAR(4)
film_has_commentaries CHAR(4)
film_has_deleted_scenes CHAR(4)
film_has_behind_the_scenes CHAR(4)
film_in_category_action CHAR(4)
film_in_category_animation CHAR(4)
film_in_category_children CHAR(4)
film_in_category_classics CHAR(4)
film_in_category_comedy CHAR(4)
film_in_category_documentary CHAR(4)
film_in_category_drama CHAR(4)
film_in_category_family CHAR(4)
film_in_category_foreign CHAR(4)
film_in_category_games CHAR(4)
film_in_category_horror CHAR(4)
film_in_category_music CHAR(4)
film_in_category_new CHAR(4)
film_in_category_scifi CHAR(4)
film_in_category_sports CHAR(4)
film_in_category_travel CHAR(4)
film_id INT(11)

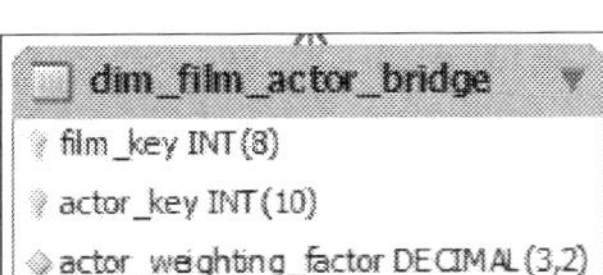
dim_film_actor_bridge
film_key INT(8)
actor_key INT(10)
actor_weighting_factor DECIMAL(3,2)

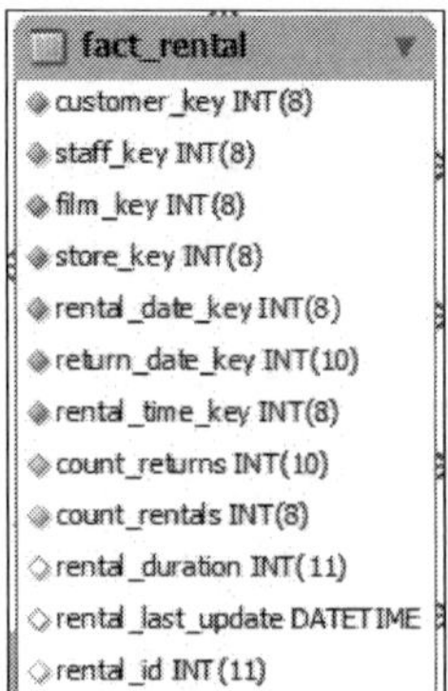
fact_rental
customer_key INT(8)
staff_key INT(8)
film_key INT(8)
store_key INT(8)
rental_date_key INT(8)
return_date_key INT(10)
rental_time_key INT(8)
count_returns INT(10)
count_rentals INT(8)
rental_duration INT(11)
rental_last_update DATETIME
rental_id INT(11)

dim_time
time_key INT(8)
time_value TIME
hours24 TINYINT(3)
hours12 TINYINT(3)
minutes TINYINT(3)
seconds TINYINT(3)
am_pm CHAR(3)

dim_date
date_key INT(8)
date_value DATE
date_short CHAR(12)
date_medium CHAR(16)
date_long CHAR(24)
date_full CHAR(32)
day_in_year SMALLINT(5)
day_in_month TINYINT(3)
is_first_day_in_month CHAR(10)
is_last_day_in_month CHAR(10)
day_abbreviation CHAR(3)
day_name CHAR(12)
week_in_year TINYINT(3)
week_in_month TINYINT(3)
is_first_day_in_week CHAR(10)
is_last_day_in_week CHAR(10)
month_number TINYINT(3)
month_abbreviation CHAR(3)
month_name CHAR(12)
year2 CHAR(2)
year4 SMALLINT(5)
quarter_name CHAR(2)
quarter_number TINYINT(3)
year_quarter CHAR(7)
year_month_number CHAR(7)
year_month_abbreviation CHAR(8)

Cognos resources

The following Cognos resources are available.

Installed Cognos manuals

The following Adobe PDF manuals are generally installed when Cognos Framework Manager is installed on your computer system:

- IBM Cognos Framework Manager Version - Guidelines for Modeling Metadata
- IBM Cognos Framework Manager Version - User Guide

Resources on the Internet

IBM Cognos Framework Manager User Guide 10.1.1 is available at `http://pic.dhe.ibm.com/infocenter/cbi/v10r1m0/index.jsp?topic=%2Fcom.ibm.swg.im.cognos.ug_fm.10.1.0.doc%2Fug_fm.htm_PD1.`

Index

Symbols

E

F

I

Q

R

S

T

U

W

Thank you for buying
IBM Cognos 10 Framework Manager

About Packt Publishing

Packt, pronounced 'packed', published its first book "Mastering phpMyAdmin for Effective MySQL Management" in April 2004 and subsequently continued to specialize in publishing highly focused books on specific technologies and solutions.

Our books and publications share the experiences of your fellow IT professionals in adapting and customizing today's systems, applications, and frameworks. Our solution based books give you the knowledge and power to customize the software and technologies you're using to get the job done. Packt books are more specific and less general than the IT books you have seen in the past. Our unique business model allows us to bring you more focused information, giving you more of what you need to know, and less of what you don't.

Packt is a modern, yet unique publishing company, which focuses on producing quality, cutting-edge books for communities of developers, administrators, and newbies alike. For more information, please visit our website: `www.packtpub.com`.

About Packt Enterprise

In 2010, Packt launched two new brands, Packt Enterprise and Packt Open Source, in order to continue its focus on specialization. This book is part of the Packt Enterprise brand, home to books published on enterprise software – software created by major vendors, including (but not limited to) IBM, Microsoft and Oracle, often for use in other corporations. Its titles will offer information relevant to a range of users of this software, including administrators, developers, architects, and end users.

Writing for Packt

We welcome all inquiries from people who are interested in authoring. Book proposals should be sent to author@packtpub.com. If your book idea is still at an early stage and you would like to discuss it first before writing a formal book proposal, contact us; one of our commissioning editors will get in touch with you.

We're not just looking for published authors; if you have strong technical skills but no writing experience, our experienced editors can help you develop a writing career, or simply get some additional reward for your expertise.

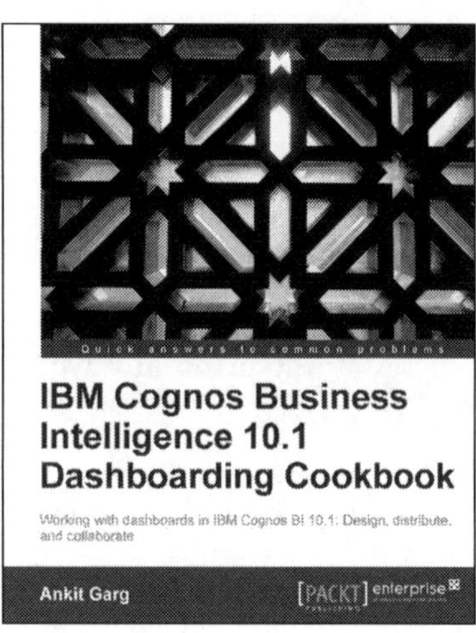

IBM Cognos Business Intelligence 10.1 Dashboarding Cookbook

ISBN: 978-1-84968-582-5 Paperback: 206 pages

Working with dashboards in IBM Cognos BI 10.1: Design, distribute, and collaborate

1. Exploring and interacting with IBM Cognos Business Insight and Business Insight Advanced
2. Creating dashboards in IBM Cognos Business Insight and Business Insight Advanced
3. Sharing and Collaborating on Dashboards using portlets

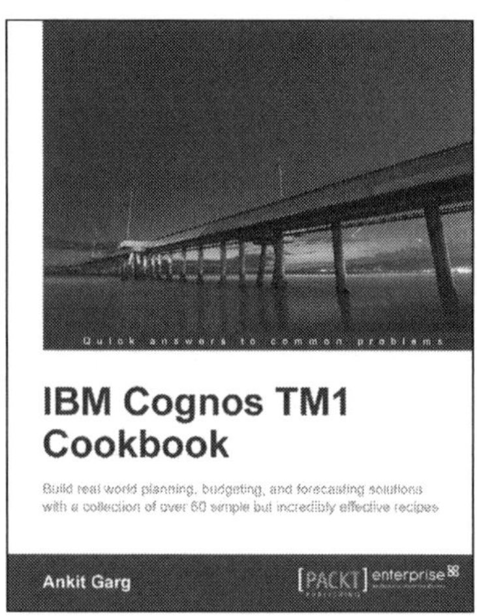

IBM Cognos TM1 Cookbook

ISBN: 978-1-84968-210-7 Paperback: 490 pages

Build real world planning, budgeting, and forecasting solutions with a collection of over 60 simple but incredibly effective recipes

1. comprehensive developer's guide for planning, building, and managing practical applications with IBM TM1
2. No prior knowledge of TM1 expected
3. Complete coverage of all the important aspects of IBM TM1 in carefully planned step-by-step practical demos
4. Part of Packt's Cookbook series: Practical recipes that illustrate the use of various TM1 features

Please check **www.PacktPub.com** for information on our titles

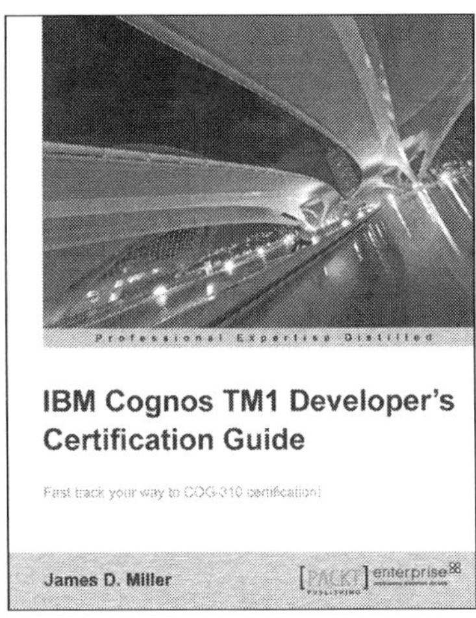

IBM Cognos TM1 Developer's Certification guide

ISBN: 978-1-84968-490-3 Paperback: 240 pages

Fast track your way to COG-310 certification!

1. Successfully clear COG-310 certification.
2. Master the major components that make up Cognos TM1 and learn the function of each.
3. Understand the advantages of using Rules versus Turbo Integrator
4. This book provides a perfect study outline and self-test for each exam topic

---

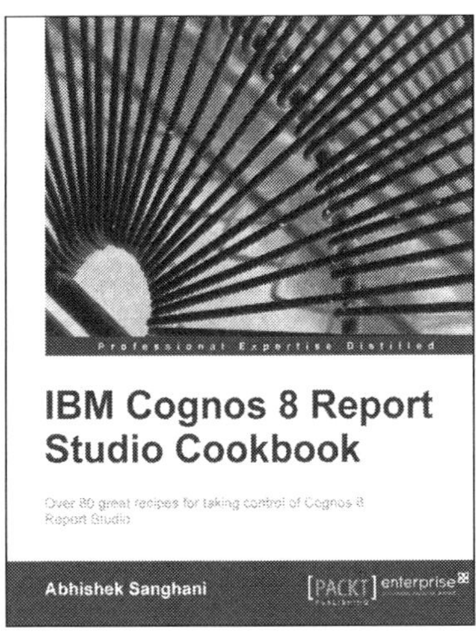

IBM Cognos 8 Report Studio Cookbook

ISBN: 978-1-84968-034-9 Paperback: 252 pages

Over 80 great recipes for taking control of Cognos 8 Report Studio

1. Learn advanced techniques to produce real-life reports that meet business demands
2. Tricks and hacks for speedy and effortless report development and to overcome tool-based limitations
3. Peek into the best practices used in industry and discern ways to work like a pro
4. Part of Packt's Cookbook series-each recipe is a carefully organized sequence of instructions to complete the task as efficiently as possible

Please check **www.PacktPub.com** for information on our titles

Made in the USA
Middletown, DE
12 August 2015